CLARENCE N. HICKMAN
THE FATHER OF
SCIENTIFIC ARCHERY

CLARENCE N. HICKMAN
THE FATHER OF
SCIENTIFIC ARCHERY

by

MARYANNE M. SCHUMM, Ed. D.

MAPLES PRESS, INC.
River Road
Minisink Hills, Pa. 18341

TO: Myrtle and Edward Miller
Marjorie and Anthony Schumm

CONTENTS

List of Illustrations

ACKNOWLEDGMENTS

The completion of this work would not have been possible without the special assistance, cooperation and support of all the contributors. To Dr. Ronald Smith, Dr. Robert Scannell, Mrs. Mary Lee Kettler, Mrs. Judy Feller, and Professor Elizabeth Koster, the writer expresses her gratitude for their suggestions, ideas and information in preparing this book.

INTRODUCTION

Two hundred people representing a wide variety of occupations, but with a common interest in the sport of archery, were gathered together in June of 1962 at Teela-Wooket Archery Camp (TWAC) in Roxbury, Vermont. They may have been interested individually in teaching or coaching the sport, improving shooting performance, making equipment, hunting, or analyzing performances from a psychological or sociological point of view. Without exception, they were extremely interested in a film, presented as part of the two-week program, entitled "The Archer's Paradox." The film, shot at 2,000 to 4,000 frames per second and made in 1937, was the first film that showed an arrow leaving a bow in slow motion. No one in that audience had ever seen the details of an arrow in motion, and the result was predictable. The film was replayed three more times. It was the 24th year that the film had been shown at TWAC, and it was this writer's first exposure to it, and to the name of its creator, Dr. Clarence N. Hickman (1889-1981), father of Scientific Archery.

Between 1963 and 1970, while serving as a TWAC staff member, the writer saw the film about a dozen times, watching with interest the awe of the audiences each time. The name Hickman continued to be mentioned often throughout the scientific portions of the programs. The writer finally decided to find out more about this person called the "Dean of TWAC," who had been to TWAC from 1938 to 1961, but not since then. In 1970, through the courtesy and efforts of Myrtle and Edward Miller, owners of TWAC, Dr. Hickman, then 81 years of age, granted an interview. The man, his keen memory, his sense of humor, his humility, and his accomplishments, was overwhelming. In 1975 the idea of documenting, in an orderly fashion, his contributions to the sport of archery was conceived and begun.

The intent of this book is to provide a description and analysis of Dr. Hickman's major scientific contributions to the sport of archery. Among the items mentioned will be his introduction of methods of scientific inquiry to the sport, the Hickman Spark Chronograph for determining arrow speed, the Hickman Shooting Machine for analysis of bows and arrows, the Hickman bow backing process, the Hickman bow of radical design, Hickman's prism bow sight, bow bracer, and his analysis of the archer's problem called "freezing."

Hickman's various occupations predisposed him with the proper technical knowledge and access to machines and materials necessary to make such noteworthy contributions to the sport. A review of his technical background and contributions in areas other than archery is presented, so one can better see the relationship between his work and his hobby, and the influence one had upon the other.

In order to better appreciate the changes Hickman made within the sport, one must have a grasp of his impact on the occupational aspects of his life. Hickman was one of those rare individuals who was successful, to a very high degree, at almost everything he attempted. The first chapter gives a brief view of his personal life, family, hobbies, and occupations. His inquisitive mind and mechanical genius helped him to become involved in such varied fields as physics, teaching, magic, mathematics, chemistry, languages, music, player pianos, rockets, weapons, and archery. He moved with apparent ease from one highly technical field to another.

Chapter two focuses more closely on selected accomplishments in those varied fields and shows the relationships among his interests and discoveries. His childhood interest in photography helped immensely in his archery and rocketry discoveries; his musical and acoustical training affected his innovations in the player piano and telephone fields. His penchant for analysis and design in technology enabled him to make a major contribution to the World War II effort. An understanding of the diversity of his background and the high level to which he perfected his understanding of each field helps one to better understand his use of those talents when persuing his favorite hobby, archery.

Chapter three presents details of Hickman's scientific inquiry into the sport of archery. It documents the need he felt to design his own testing machines and procedures, as none was available for his truly pioneering efforts. Also highlighted are some of the more than thirty-five scientific articles written for archery magazines as well as a description of his bow of radical design. Additional technological innovations are explained in chapter four, including his process for applying backing to bows, his bow weighing machine, and his high speed motion pictures of an arrow leaving a bow.

Hickman's contributions to the sport were not limited to the technical aspects. He founded many clubs, held offices in others, organized the first international telegraphic archery competition, served as the

Dean of the only archery training center in the world for 43 years, and was a catalyst and role model for others in the sport. These administrative efforts are covered in chapter five.

Most of Hickman's seventy years in archery were filled with the joys of contributing new ideas, shooting with friends, and helping others learn. There was, however, a period of time --13 long years -- when Hickman refused to touch a bow, attend a tournament, or teach at TWAC. This was surely the most trying period of his life. Chapter six explains Hickman's loneliness, frustration, and bitterness that ensued from rules and structural changes within the organizing body of the sport, the National Archery Association.

The theme of this biography is that the application of the technological genius of Clarence Hickman to the sport of archery transformed archery from an art to a science. It may be no exaggeration to state that Hickman was the twentieth century's Leonardo Da Vinci in the field of archery. Technology and archery met in the mind and hands of Hickman — archery has not since been the same.

CHAPTER

I

CLARENCE N. HICKMAN -- BIOGRAPHICAL SKETCH

Fig. 2 (1978)

Fig. 1 (1951)

It might seem unusual for a boy born on a simple rural farm in Indiana to achieve national distinction in a diversity of highly technical fields. A closer look at some of the background events in Clarence Hickman's life makes it seem almost natural that this talented and creative individual would make contributions in such diverse fields as rocketry, photography, music, communications, and archery. Clarence Nichols Hickman was born August 16, 1889 on a farm about one mile north of Lizton, Indiana. He had three older brothers, William, born in 1881, George, born in 1884, and Hanson, born in 1887, and one younger sister, Ruth, born in 1892. His parents, James Willis and Lucinda Leak Hickman, were married December 31, 1873. Both parents came from farming families, and Hickman's father owned and worked on a farm. His father was mechanically inclined and excelled at carpentry. It was his love of hunting and fishing with bow and arrow which would greatly influence young Hickman. Hickman's father went to school two terms at Lagoda Academy in Indiana and later attended a teacher training school, Central Normal College, near Danville, Indiana during the Civil War, often walking twelve miles one way.[1]

At an early age, Clarence Hickman's varied interests became apparent. He started school at age six, attending Leak Country School in Hendrick's County, Indiana, about a mile from the farm. At this age he began to shoot a bow, and he also became interested in magic, having seen a show in Lizton where some magic was performed. He never lost his keen interest in magic and in later life was a professional magician for a short time. When he was nine, in 1898, Hickman attended No. 8 school, farther north of Lizton. At about this time he displayed some of his mechanical ability and became interested in repairing watches. This later developed into a hobby, and he often repaired watches for friends. He also became interested in fishing and shooting fish with a bow and arrow, influenced by his father and older brothers.[2]

Since Hickman came from a large, relatively poor family, he became enterprising early in life to obtain the things he wanted. When he was eleven, the family moved to a farm west of Jamestown, Indiana. During the year he received a two by two inch cardboard camera when he subscribed to the *Chicago Ledger*. His interest in photography became so keen that he cut and shucked corn to earn enough money to buy a three and a half inch camera. He then began to charge for the pictures that he took.[3]

Hickman continued to develop his talents after his family bought a 240 acre farm four and a half miles north of Martinsville, Indiana. Hickman, at age 14, attended the Dyer Country School about one mile from the farm. During this time in the early 1900's, he continued to do photographic work, and also studied the cornet and guitar, teaching himself to play and read music. He and his oldest brother, who played the violin, often earned money by playing for country square dances. They even cut hickory poles for the Old Hickory Chair Factory at Martinsville. To earn money for photographic supplies, Hickman cleaned the school house and tended the fire for ten cents a day. He also added to his personal income by raising and selling tomatoes.[4]

In June 1904, Hickman graduated from eighth grade. Because he was needed on the farm he was not able to begin ninth grade at the high school, which was located almost five miles away. Rather than miss school, which he enjoyed, he repeated eighth grade. Using his mathematical and mechanical abilities, Hickman surveyed and built an open ditch for his father using a square and level. His father did not have much confidence in his son's "civil engineering," claiming that the water was going to run backwards. When the first big rain came, his father went out to see how the ditch was working and was surprised but happy to see that the water was running in the right direction.[5]

Hickman's mother recognized her son's abilities and was upset that he was going to be deprived of a high school education. She persuaded her husband to sell the farm and move back west of Jamestown to a rented farm. As Hickman pursued his high school education, he independently took up the study of German, using only books for study. He would translate his Latin into German and sometimes into Spanish, and then into English. Often he would study German in the fields while taking a break from farm chores, much to his father's dismay. His father could not understand why he would be interested in studying German. Besides academic pursuits, he continued his interest in photography, becoming the official photographer for the Standard Oil Company, which was erecting a pumping station at Jamestown. His job was to take pictures for progress reports. He continued playing the guitar, and renewed his interest in magic. He presented two magic shows, one at Jamestown and another later at Brownsburg.[6]

When Hickman returned to Jamestown, he renewed his friendship with Stanley Hendricks, the owner of the photography store from which he had purchased his supplies. Hendricks had given up the photographic business and bought a clothing store in Jamestown. Hendricks hired the seventeen year old Hickman to clerk in his clothing store on Saturdays and during the summer of 1906. With this money, Hickman was able to buy a good eight by ten inch camera with all the accessories. He continued to earn money taking photographs. Soon, though, the family moved again: late in 1906 they bought an eighty acre farm about one mile south of Jamestown. The farmhouse had eight rooms, the largest in which they had ever lived. By then Hickman's oldest brother William had married and moved, and Hanson had become Superintendent of Schools in the Phillipine Islands.[7]

Although Hickman was not afraid of physical labor, it soon became obvious that he was not destined to become a farmer. Hickman described how his ingenuity solved one problem but created another, while doing some work on his parent's new farm:

> The summer after I had finished my junior year of high school, I was sowing wheat in a corn field. This we did with a drill pulled by one horse. To keep the horse from stopping and nipping off blades of corn, I put a muzzle on him. However, he was a big horse and the corn was tall and had very large and heavy blades so as the horse went forward the blades would slide off the horse and

hit me in the face. My face was rather tender and I could not take it so I went into the barn and got a horse muzzle and fitted it to my face to act as a guard. It worked fine except for one thing. My father came out and saw me with the muzzle and he raised the roof. He called me a sissy and many other names. It hurt pretty badly but I did not lose my temper. However, I made up my mind that I was going to continue to use the muzzle. It so happened that when I stopped for lunch that the mail man brought a letter for me from Stan Hendricks. In the letter he offered to let me attend the Waynetown High School and work in his store mornings, noon and evenings, and of course Saturdays. I also was to agree to work for him the following summer. I took the first train to Waynetown and he offered me $6 per week during the school period and $9 per week for the summer work. I accepted. There were no hard feelings on the part of my father or myself. I think he had concluded that I would never make a good farmer.[8]

In the fall of 1908, Hickman went to Waynetown to clerk in Hendricks' store full time and to finish high school. He graduated from high school in 1909, and at the end of school, he made a short tour of opera houses in Indiana as a professional magician. He then informed Hendricks that he wanted to go to college. That fall, Hendricks had a big sale and sold out most of the store, so he suggested that Hickman take the winter off and pursue a normal teacher's course. Hickman did that, attending Winona College, Winona Lake, Indiana, for four months, where he took such courses as geography, geology, mathematics, and classroom management.[9]

After four months of schooling Hickman was offered a job teaching seventh and eighth grades in the Waynetown Public Schools for $45 per month. Hickman spoke of this first job with typical humor "I never knew whether the chairman of the school board thought I would be a good teacher or if he just wanted to keep me in town to board and room at his sister's place."[10] During the first year of teaching, Hickman organized a band at the school, and by spring they were all playing well enough to perform in public. It was at this time that he began to play the clarinet, which was later to play an important part in his life.

After his first year of teaching, Hickman spent the summer touring as a professional magician, billed as "The Hoosier Magician" (See Appendix A & B). He performed in opera houses and churches, demonstrating tricks and illusions he had devised. The following year, 1911-12, Hickman was offered twice his salary to teach in the Jamestown High School, provided he could teach German as well as mathematics and science. He took the state examinations in German, passed, and got the job. Hickman's father, who had scolded him for studying German on the farm, was very proud of him for obtaining this job at $84 per month.

Hickman continued to pursue his formal education. He worked toward his B.A. degree at Winona College while teaching mathematics and science at Jamestown. He completed his degree in 1914, continuing to teach physics at the college during the winter, and surveying and mathematics during the summer.[11]

With degree in hand, he took a job teaching physics and mathematics at New Albany, High School in Indiana for $900 the first year, 1914, and $1000 the next two years. While there, he roomed at the home of William Bigwood, and eventually became engaged to Bigwood's daughter, Mabel. They shared an interest in music and played duets together every evening, she on the piano and he on the clarinet. They were married on July 17, 1915, and Hickman continued to teach at Winona College in the summers and New Albany during the year.[12]

Hickman's desire to continue work in the sciences led him to apply to the master's degree program at Clark University in Worcester, Massachusetts. He studied for admission during the summer of 1917 as America entered World War I, and was accepted for the fall of 1917. The time spent at Clark University was to affect Hickman's entire career. Although he was already deeply involved with physics, he was about to become associated with Dr. Robert Goddard, the great physicist and engineer, who laid the foundation for America's development in rockets, missiles, earth satellites, and space flight. This association would turn his career away from teaching and into research. Hickman's description of this first meeting is both humble and humorous, yet as a result of this meeting he was ultimately to solve one of Goddard's greatest problems:

> During the year I met Dr. Robert H. Goddard, who was head of the college physics department. There were two schools at that time. I was in the graduate school with Dr. G. Stanley Hall as president and Dr. Arthur Gordon Webster was head of the graduate physics department. Dr. Goddard was at that time working on the development of rockets and was having trouble getting good results. He was trying to develop a rocket that used the same combustion chamber by feeding in successive charges of cordite powder. The man working for him was trying to use the breech block system but the residue from the powder would clog the mechanism so that in a whole year they had not succeeded in getting the lock to open without the use of wrenches. He spoke to Dr. L.T.E. Thompson, who was Dr. Webster's assistant. Dr. Thompson told him that he would recommend that he talk to C.N. Hickman who had come to them recommended as being unusually good in mechanical designs. Dr. Goddard took his advice and talked to me. I told him that I thought he was trying to do almost the impossible. However, he asked me to give the matter some consideration. This I promised to do and that evening I gave the

matter some thought, and the more I thought of it the more difficult I thought it would be to do what he was trying to do. I finally gave up the job and went to my own studies for the evening. During my thoughts on the problem I had not arrived at a single suggestion of how it might be done. I went to bed with no further thoughts on the subject. That night I had a vivid dream of a solution to his problem. Knowing that I would not remember it the next morning, I slipped out of bed and went into the living room and began making sketches of the plan. My wife missed me and came out to see what was the matter. She asked me if I were ill. I told her I was not ill and was making some sketches before I forgot the dream. She then said...'Well! You may not be sick but you sure are crazy!'[13]

Hickman showed his sketches to Goddard the next day, and Goddard was impressed. He requested that Hickman work with him for the rest of the year and join him in his research after he received his degree. Although Hickman had expected to return to teaching, Goddard offered him $200 per month which was more than he would be earning in the teaching field. The next year Goddard moved his laboratory from Worcester, Massachusetts to the Mount Wilson Observatory Shops in Pasadena, California. After receiving his M.A. degree, Hickman joined Goddard on July 3, 1918. They immediately began work on Hickman's idea, which was to feed charges in through the tail of the combustion chamber instead of through a breech block, eliminating the problem of the mechanism clogging up. Hickman described the process in this way:

> The front of each charge had a percussion cap that, after being shot into the chamber with a spring actuated by the recoil, would hit a firing pin located in the head of the chamber. This ignited the charge and this was repeated for as many times as there were charges shot into the chamber. In about one week we had our first test and we fired three charges and a dummy into the chamber. The big problem was to provide a mechanism that would feed several hundred charges into the chamber. It was not difficult to take care of several charges, but to provide the required number it proved very difficult.[14]

Ultimately Hickman and Goddard decided to put their efforts into developing a single charge rocket, rather than experimenting with multiple charge rockets. While the meeting with Goddard was to profoundly affect his career choice, an incident which occurred caused Hickman to readjust physically to many of the things he enjoyed doing. On August 18, 1918, an accident in the lab caused Hickman to lose several of his fingers. He had been working with a six-charge rocket, and on this occasion only two of the charges fired. In recalling the incident Hickman explained:

On examination I found that the third charge was in the combustion chamber but the paper cover at the end of the charge had been pierced by the firing pin. I made the mistake of thinking that I had forgotten to put in the percussion cap and when I went to tear the paper off the charge went off in my hands. I lost several fingers in the accident but Dr. Goddard hired a lad from Cal Tech School to work under my directions until my hands were healed.[15]

Hickman was extremely thankful that his eyes had been unharmed by the blast, especially since most of his face had been hit and burned by bits of powder. The surgeon did a fine job with his fingers, and he missed only about a day of work due to the accident. He spent very little time mourning the loss of his fingers. He lost the distal portions of the thumb, the first two fingers on the left hand, and the distal portion of the first finger on the right hand. His biggest regret was that the missing parts prevented him from playing his clarinet.[16]

Hickman was determined that the accident would not affect his ability to work with Dr. Goddard. He began to work on the concept of a single charge rocket fired from a tube, called a recoilless gun. It could be fired at a close range on the shoulder, or for distance, under the arm. It was called the Bazooka during World War II.[17]

Goddard and Hickman went to the Aberdeen Proving Grounds in Maryland in the fall of 1918 to demonstrate the rockets they had developed. Hickman had charge of the recoilless gun and the multiple charge rocket, plus a three inch rocket to be fired from planes. While they were there, World War I ended, but Goddard was confident that he could obtain funds to continue rocket work. He pursuaded Hickman again not to return to teaching but promised to help him get a job from which he could be released when the funds became available to continue the rocket work. He arranged for Hickman to work with the Bureau of Standards in the Inductance and Capacitance Laboratory in Washington, D.C., starting in 1919. Soon after, Goddard found that he would not receive any further funding for rocket work.[18]

Hickman was now on his way toward working through a variety of jobs, each of which would call forth his remarkable abilities. He stayed at the Bureau of Standards for a short period, and during that time his only child, Mary Lee, was born on June 8, 1919, in New Albany, Indiana.* In 1920, Hickman was again pursuaded to change his job. Dr. L. Thomp-

---

*She was later to follow in her father's footsteps and become a physicist. She received her M.S. at University of Michigan and taught physics at Colby Jr. College in New Hampshire, Brooklyn College, and Columbia University. She also taught acoustics at the Juilliard School of Music.[19]

son, Assistant Director of Physics at Clark University, organized the Industrial Research Laboratores to do work for commercial concerns. The directors included Dr. Thompson, Dr. Goddard, Mr. Hickman and Mr. Nils Riffolt. They did analysis work for companies such as The Winchester Arms Company, LaFrance Fire Engine Company, and Witherbee Ignitere Company, until 1921. At that time a recession began and commercial funding ceased.[20]

Hickman, meanwhile, was working on his doctorate at Clark University. He returned to the Bureau of Standards in the Inductance and Capacitance Laboratory, and he also did some work for the Navy. While he was working at the Bureau, he wrote a paper on the alternating current resistance and inductance of single layer coils, confirming laboratory measurements.[21] It was published and accepted by Clark University as his dissertation for the doctorate in 1922.[22]

Upon receipt of his degree, the Bureau of Standards offered to raise his salary from $1800 to $2000 per year; however, the Naval Ordnance offered him $4400 to work at the Bureau of Mines Research Testing group in the Washington Navy Yard. Hickman spent the next several years developing submarine mines.[23]

His employment at the Bureau of Mines was short-lived, for in 1924, Charles Fuller Stoddard, the inventor of the AMPICO Reproducing Piano, went to the Bureau of Standards to get recommendations for a physicist who might work with his company. Dr. F.C. Brown, the Assistant Director of the Bureau, recommended Hickman. The Research Laboratory of the American Piano Company in New York City offered Hickman $7500. Hickman accepted this offer and terminated his employment at the Bureau of Mines. He quickly develped a system to measure the loudness of a tone as played by an artist, and was personally responsible for developing the AMPICO B Reproducing Piano. The Laboratory raised his salary to $10,000 and made it retroactive for an entire year.[24]

While working at the piano company, Hickman began to do research on designing better bows for archery, another of his hobbies. Using the piano laboratory for his experiments, he published many papers regarding his investigations. He was active in many archery clubs and was instrumental in starting several others. His continuing experiments and articles were to earn him the title, "Father of Scientific Archery." His outstanding contributions in this area will be covered later.

Hickman was again destined to change jobs. When the stock market crashed in 1929, the American Piano Company, which had been sold to the Bankers Trust Company, went into the hands of receivers. On January 1, 1930, Hickman accepted a job at the New York branch of Bell Telephone Laboratories. His first assignment with the Bell Laboratories was to work on magnetic recording. At that time, Bell Labs had a machine that recorded on piano wire, but its quality was poor, and it had very little range above the background noise. Hickman substituted steel tape for wire and greatly increased the range above the noise. The wire machine fed wire through at about three feet per second, and the tape was able to reduce the speed to one foot per second. In a short time the volume range was increased from twelve to seventy decibels. Many company officials thought this was a waste of time, for they were not able to foresee the modern tape recorder.[25] In addition to magnetic recording improvements, Hickman spent some time in the Acoustical Department, helping develop devices for measuring and showing speech patterns. Later, in the 30's he was transferred to the machine switching group which was working on new ways of doing machine switching in central offices.[26]

One of the most distinguished assignments of Hickman's career came around 1940, when hostilities in Europe were escalating. With prophetic accuracy, Hickman foresaw the need for rocket development to aid in the war effort. He was almost singlehandedly responsible for involving the United States in its rocket development efforts. Hickman sent a letter to Dr. Frank Jewett, head of Bell Laboratories and also president of the National Academy of Science. He convinced him of the military uses of rockets and the necessity for rocket development. It was Hickman's letter that resulted in the program that provided America's rocket weapons for World War II.[27] Hickman was placed in charge of Section H (for Hickman) of Division A, National Defense Research Committee (NDRC). As the war progressed, Hickman spent less and less time at Bell Laboratories and more time working for the government. His own statements indicate the diversity of his contributions:

> The Bell Labs paid my salary and the NDRC paid my expenses. By the time the war ended I was spending one day per week at the Bell Labs and the rest of the time at the NDRC....In addition to administrative work connected with U.S. Rocket Developments. I did lots of design and inventive work on rockets, recoilless guns, flame throwers, bazooka rockets, airplane rockets. I developed an 8mm 6,000 frame per second movie camera for photographing rockets in flight. This was followed by the development of a Ribbon Frame camera that took the place of the movie camera, the camera being quite portable. Some weeks I spent as many as 90 hours on my work and travelled all over the country.[28]

After the war, Hickman continued to work at Bell Laboratories, until January 1, 1950, when he retired. During this time at Bell, he continued his avid interest in archery, using Bell Laboratories for experiments. He wrote over 34 archery articles and was active in shooting and forming archery clubs. Hickman founded a Bell Labs Archery Club at each of the branches. He also served as Dean of Teela-Wooket Archery Camp, in Vermont, later known as The World Archery Center.

In June 1950, when the Korean War erupted, he was requested by Dr. Quarles, one of the Bell Laboratories Vice-Presidents to assist the Sandia Corporation, at Albuquerque, New Mexico, in the marriage program of atomic warheads to guided missiles. He planned to stay just one year, but enjoyed the country so much he remained until 1953. Hickman would have preferred to remain in the West, but his wife preferred New York, so they returned to their Jackson Heights apartment.[29] The Sandia Corporation continued to call upon Hickman as a consultant until 1958, when he submitted his last bill.

From 1958 to 1963, Hickman spent his time on retirement activities, mostly archery, fishing, and magic. He continued to shoot, write articles, and invent archery aids. An event which occurred within the National Archery Association in 1961 was to sour him on archery for many years: Hickman's status as an amateur archer was questioned, a story to be recounted in greater detail later.

While in retirement, an illness to his wife, Mabel, affected Hickman greatly. She developed arteriosclerosis of the brain, which caused hallucinations and early senility. Although he tried to take care of her at home, she had to be institutionalized in 1964, passing away in 1965. In each of the documents written after his wife's death, Hickman stated that life no longer meant anything to him. He was so devastated he felt he probably would not live more than a year or two afer his wife. With this as a catalyst, he began work on a genealogy of the Hickman families, to be passed on to his daughter and heirs. He spent the summers in Jackson Heights and the winters in Florida, with his sister Ruth. His mental health gradually returned with the challenge of the task, and he finished the work in 1967.

In the *Genealogy,* in a section on his life, he presented interesting comments on the subject of dreams, and how they affected his life:

> I have never been able to explain the dream that catapaulted me into research on rockets. All my life I have dreamed a great deal but only on three occasions have the dreams had much effect on my life. The dream of a solution to Dr. Goddard's rocket problem undoubtedly had a big effect on my life.
>
> After having the accident at Pasadena where I lost several fingers, I sold my clarinets, thinking that I would no longer be able to play them. However, I began to have dreams that I could still play the clarinet. These dreams persisted for over ten years. Finally, when I was at the Research Laboratory of the American Piano Com-

pany, I went to the Wurlitzer Company to see if they could modify
a clarinet so that I could play it. When they saw my hands, they
laughed at me, saying that it was impossible. The dreams persisted and I then went to see a young man whom I had met in our
laboratory. He was a clerk in a music house on 14th St. I put the
problem to him and he said they could not do the job but suggested that I do the modification. He said . . . 'You are a good
mechanic and you have excellent tools in your laboratory.' I had
never thought of doing this, but it sounded reasonable to me, so I
bought a clarinet and he gave me a box of old keys. On a weekend
I did the job. When the job was completed, I was amazed to find
that after a period of ten years I could still play and found to my
utter amazement that I could still read music. I immediately purchased a B flat instrument and modified it, making several improvements in the method of modification. At this time I had
begun to have difficulties in deep breathing and did not feel so
well. After a short time of playing the clarinet, my breathing difficulties disappeared and I felt better. I got a great deal of
pleasure out of playing the instrument. When I got deep into
World War II rocket activities, I no longer had the time to play
the clarinets and I put them in our closet. After the war was over,
I began to have dreams that the clarinets were cracked. This did
not seem reasonable to me for I have always taken excellent care
of my instruments. The dreams persisted and finally out of
curiosity I got the clarinets out of the closet and found that they
were in excellent condition. However, I began to play
again...thinking that I might again help my breathing difficulties
which had returned. It did cure the difficulty and since that time I
often play the clarinet to insure deep breathing.[30]

He continued to play the clarinet even after he had a double cataract
operation. His other hobbies continued to be an important part of his
life, including work on magic tricks, attending The World Archery
Center, watch and clock repair, work on jewelry, and organizing his files.

Between 1971 and 1981 he led a quiet life, travelling to Florida
each year, but was limited in his writing and reading by his still failing
eyesight. He still made speeches in the different areas of his expertise,
entertained with magic tricks, and walked two miles daily besides pursu-
ing an exercise program. He was the recipient of numerous honors and
awards, and in 1977 he was inducted into both the New York State and
National Archery Association Halls of Fame.

Hickman's statements about his life were the same in 1967,[31] as they
were in 1979.[32]

I have had an interesting and active life. Up until 1963, when my
wife became ill, we had very little illness in the immediate family.
I believe that our trials and tribulations , for the most part, were
below average for such a family. I have never regretted having

15

had so many different occupations. I probably could have been better at one particular job but my life would not have been so rich.[33]

Clarence Hickman died of a heart attack in the garden of his apartment in Jackson Heights on May 7, 1981, at the age of 92.

The following pages will document in more detail the versatility and genius of Clarence Hickman throughout his more than seventy productive years. Although the focus will be on his contributions to the field of archery, various aspects of his work will be analyzed, so the true range of his abilities may be better appreciated.

Fig. 3

Clarence Hickman's 85th Birthday, August, 1974. Hickman, on the clarinet, is accompanied by Myrtle Miller, Director of The World Archery Center, and her brother Chris Kutchinski.[34]

REFERENCES

1. Clarence N. Hickman, *Genealogy of the Hickman Families of Virginia, Kentucky, Indiana and Texas*, (Jackson Heights, N.Y.: Westminster Printing Co., 1967), p.46

2. Clarence N. Hickman, "Highlights in the Life of Clarence N. Hickman," October 15, 1980, 9 page letter, Hickman Archives, p.1.

3. Clarence N. Hickman, Letter to Dr. Harvey Fletcher, February 3, 1965, 17 pages, Hickman Archives, p.1.

4. Hickman, *Genealogy*, p.46.

5. *Ibid.*, p.47.

6. Hickman, letter to Dr. Fletcher, p.2.

7. Hickman, *Genealogy*, p.47.

8. Hickman, letter to Dr. Fletcher, p.3.

9. Hickman, "Highlights," p.2.

10. Hickman, letter to Dr. Fletcher, p.3.

11. Hickman, *Genealogy*, p.48.

12. *Ibid.*, p.48

13. *Ibid.*, p.49

14. *Ibid.*, p.50

15. Hickman, "Highlights," p.6.

16. Hickman, letter to Dr. Fletcher, p.13.

17. Hickman, *Genealogy*, p.50.

18. Hickman, "Highlights," p.7.

19. Hickman, *Genealogy*, p.25.

20. Hickman, "Highlights," p.21.

21. Clarence N. Hickman, "Alternating-Current Resistance and Inductance of Single-Layer Coils." *Scientific Papers of the Bureau of Standards*, Department of Commerce, Washington, D.C., 1923, pp.73-104, Hickman Archives.

22. Hickman, "Highlights," p.7.

23. *Ibid.*, p.7.

24. *Ibid.*, p.7.

25. *Ibid.*, p.8.

26. Hickman, *Genealogy*, p.51.

27. Joint Board on Scientific Information Policy, Office of Scientific Research and Development, War Department and Navy Department, *U.S. Rocket Ordnance--Development and Use in World War II*, March 30, 1946, p.10, Hickman Archives.

28. Hickman, *Genealogy*, p.52.

29. *Ibid.*, p.54.

30. *Ibid.*, p.56-57.
31. *Ibid.*, p.56.
32. Interview with Clarence N. Hickman, Jackson Heights, N.Y., September 10, 1979.
33. Hickman, *Genealogy*, p.56.
34. C.N. Hickman, "Clarence N. Hickman's 85th birthday and Christian D. Kutchinski's 52nd Wedding Anniversary" August 18, 1974, Hickman Archives.

Fig. 4

Artist's Sketch of Clarence Hickman
Depicting His Various Accomplishments

CLARENCE N. HICKMAN -- INVENTOR

Hickman was a genius in the application of science to archery, but he was certainly not limited to archery inventions. His inventive talents covered areas such as photography, communications, rocketry, ballistics, magic, and music. His forte seemed to be mechanical design. He was extremely adept at looking at a mechanical problem and solving it with seemingly very little effort. Each of his occupations and avocational interests resulted in inventions and innovations. A complete list of his patents appears in Appendix C & D.

Hickman's life as a researcher began with his association with Robert Goddard. Although he worked with Goddard only a short time, his experiments with rockets, recoilless guns, and ballistics during World War I greatly influenced his future contributions in World War II. With the close of World War I and the end of funding for Goddard's work, Hickman planned to return to teaching, which he enjoyed. Goddard persuaded him to do otherwise and to get involved in work from which he could be released if the funding could be renewed.

Hickman was employed by the Bureau of Standards in Washington, D.C. from 1919 to 1920 and from 1921 to 1922. During the time he was working on his doctorate at Clark University, he published a paper for the Bureau that was accepted as his dissertation. The paper, "Alternating-Current Resistance and Inductance of Single-Layer Coils," was basically a mathematical treatise attempting to apply an integral equation method to single-layer coils.[1] Hickman also published another paper while working for the Bureau, entitled "A Variable Resistor of Low Value."[2] Resistors were used for making electrical measurements, and the ones in use at the time employed copper wire and mercury. They proved ineffective for making measurements needing a high degree of accuracy, due to the high temperature coefficient of mercury. In addition, when careful measurements needed to be made, the continual change of resistance due to the heat factor made mercury unsuitable for carrying large currents. Hickman devised an improved resistor utilizing manganin, which has a higher resistance than the mercury. (Fig. 5)

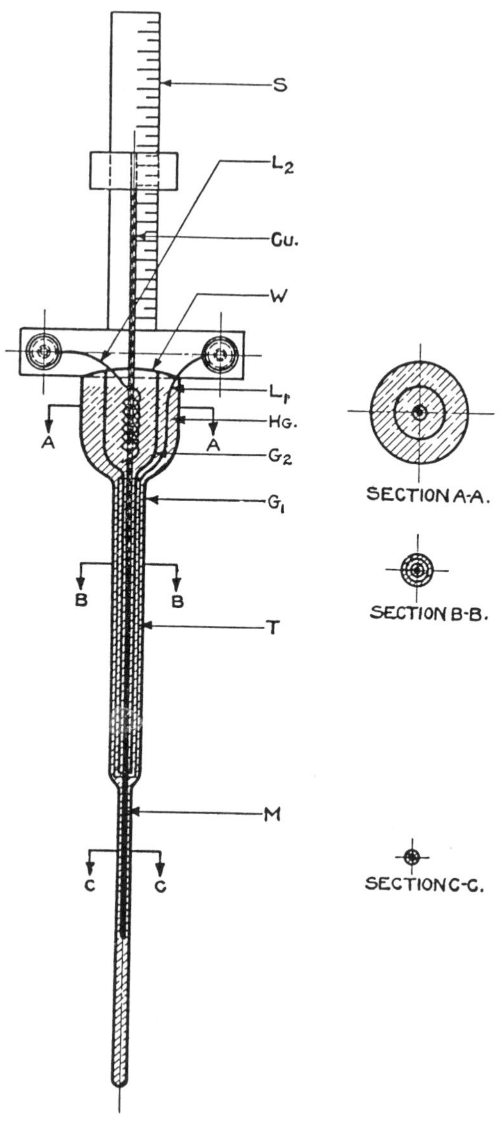

Fig. 5

(Oct., 1922)   MANGANIN SLIDE RESISTOR

In 1920-21, Hickman spent a year working as a director of the Industrial Research Corporation at Clark University. The purpose of the corporation was to do research and analysis for industrial firms. One of the companies utilizing the services of the corporation was Winchester Arms. Hickman never lost his interest in photography, and utilized spark photographs to take pictures of shots from different bore guns, determining the longitudinal despersion for distances up to twenty yards. The following photograph shows the spark apparatus used for testing the shotgun charge, and the diagram shows the wiring of the apparatus. (Fig. 6,7)

Fig. 6   Spark Apparatus For Testing Shotgun Charge

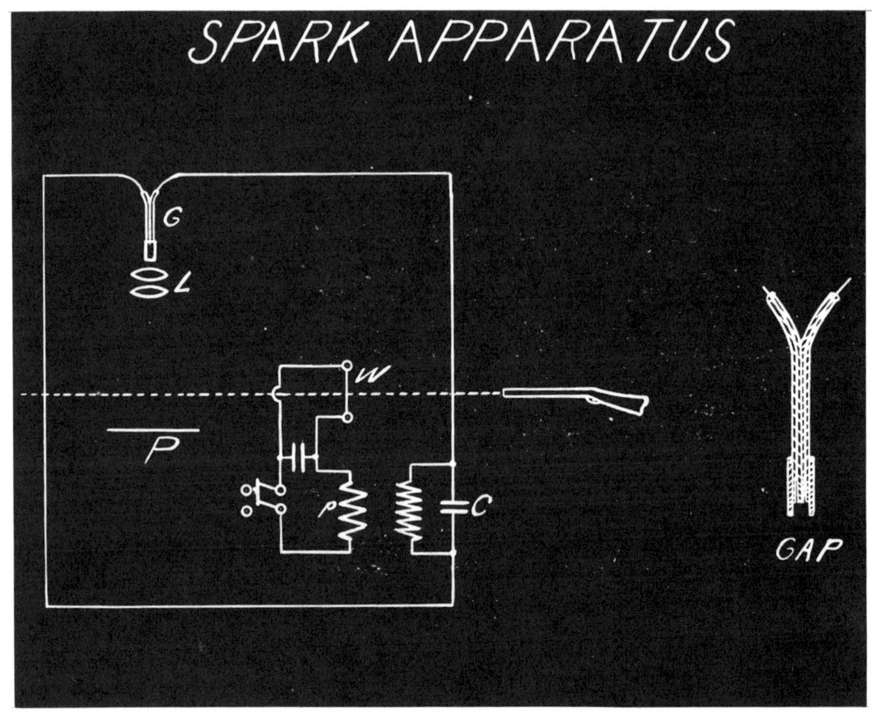

Fig. 7   Sketch of Wiring of Spark Apparatus

Hickman was quite proud of several problems he had solved, but despite the efficiency of each solution, he was praised by company officials for only one. Winchester Arms had a rifle which they claimed would not shoot where it was aimed. Each time they clamped the rifle in a vice and fired it, it would shoot low. Claiming that it was the vibration of the barrel that caused the problem, they were prepared to spend $1,000,000 to re-tool the process of making the barrel and end the vibration. The Industrial Research Corporation, specifically Hickman, was given the job of proving that it was a faulty barrel. Hickman solved the problem in this way:

> I set up a gun in a vice and by means of tipping a mirror that sent a beam of light on to a rotating drum with photographic film, I set it so that the beam of light was focused on the slit in the drum. I cocked the hammer and fired the gun and got no beam of light on the film at all. I tried again but noticed this time that when I cocked the hammer that the beam of light was thrown out of the slit. I reset the beam with the hammer cocked so that it was hitting the slit of the drum and got the record and it showed that there was no vibration of the barrel until after the bullet had left the gun. They then discovered that the spring that actuated the ham-

mer had one end attached to the gun stock so in cocking the hammer this stress caused the barrel to tip. They were delighted with my tests and I got lots of praise for that test.[3]

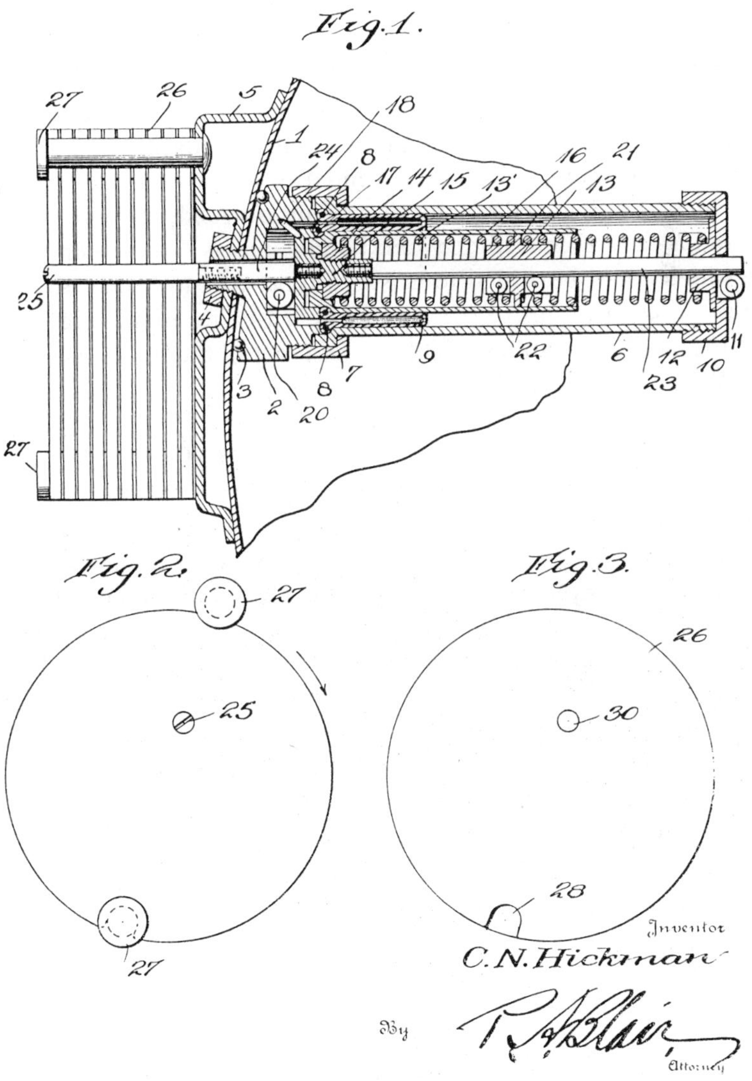

Fig. 8 - Schematic of Submarine Mine

Another test involved the chokes on different guns, but the company felt differently about the results. After much experimentation, Hickman decided that it was unnecessary to have different guns with different chokes, and he designed an attachment that could be put on any gun. With the attachment one could get any choke desired, and the cost of the device was relatively small. "I expected to get lots of praise for this invention," stated Hickman, "but all I got was HELL for they wanted to sell several guns to a hunter instead of the one with a few attachments. I understand that such a device is now on the market."[4]

Hickman returned to the Bureau of Standards for a year, after an absence of funding closed down the Research Corporation. The Bureau of Mines then lured him away with a salary increase. He spent two years with the Bureau of Mines, working mostly with submarine mines. During his short tenure there, Hickman invented an improved self-calibrating mine, which was dropped by the ship being pursued. It came to rest in the water at a pre-determined depth. Hickman's patent concerned a device which could be added to existing mines to allow them to become self-calibrating, or improve the process of self-calibration. (Fig. 8)[5]

In 1924 Charles Fuller Stoddard, designer of the Ampico reproducing piano for the American Piano Company of New York, decided he needed a physicist in his lab to help with design changes he wished to make. He lured Hickman away from the Bureau of Mines by doubling his salary. With the convenience of a well equipped lab and the freedom to pursue investigations, Hickman soon became immersed in research work for the reproducing piano. (Fig. 9) The reproducing pianos were quite different from player pianos. Reproducing pianos could faithfully reproduce the piece of music as played by the artist, by using specially recorded music rolls. With the aid of controlling perforations on the rolls, the full range of the piano could be duplicated, including accenting, diminuendo and crescendo, and even half-pedaling. Since the phonograph was not highly developed at this particular time, the reproducing piano was the most sought after instrument of those who valued fine music interpretation. (Fig. 10)[6]

Larry Givens, an expert on the history of the reproducing piano, and the author of the book, *Re-enacting the Artist*, stated that Hickman's term of service with the American Piano Company from 1924-1929 was the only period in the history of the player piano where real scientific investigation and methodology were applied to the development of the piano. Previously the developments had been trial and error, but Hickman brought a high degree of sophistication to player piano technology.[7]

Hickman is credited with at least a half dozen developments for the

Entire Piano Industry to Profit by Work of Newly Organized Research Department of American Piano Co.

To Promote Advancement in the Artistic Side of Piano Manufacture, Is High Purpose of American Piano Co.—Findings of Leading Scientific Experts to Be Made Public—Personnel of Department Now Includes Charles F. Stoddard, C. N. Hickman, Ph.D., and John Anderson

Fig. 9 Personnel of the New Research Department of the American Piano Co.: Charles F. Stoddard (Center), C.N. Hickman, Ph.D. (Left) and John Anderson (Right)

player piano, most of which were responsible for the birth of the AM-PICO B model piano, considered by many to be the most sophisticated form of reproducing piano. Prior to Hickman's arrival at the piano company, the method of recording the notes played by the artists was adequate. However, there was no way to record the dynamics of the performance. Dynamics were inserted later by editors, who would guess at the accents intended. In the mid-1920's, Hickman designed a machine for recording dynamics of performances. It operated on the principle of a spark chronograph and measured with great accuracy the velocity of the piano hammers during their last half inch of travel toward the strings. Since Hickman needed a spark chronograph that would record at low voltage and with low paper speed, he designed what was necessary. His paper "Spark Chronograph Developed for Measuring Intensity of Percussion Instrument Tones" was published in 1929.[8] With the advent of this recording device, it was no longer necessary for humans to guess how the artist meant a note to be played. After a long series of steps from the recording of the piece to the production of the final note sheet, the note sheet was placed on a special stencil machine in the Ampico labs. The machine, using the original note sheet, produced a playable copy of the roll, with expression. As originally designed by Stoddard, the complex action of this stencil machine required seven valves per note. Dr. Hickman reduced this to four valves per note, making the entire operation more efficient.[9]

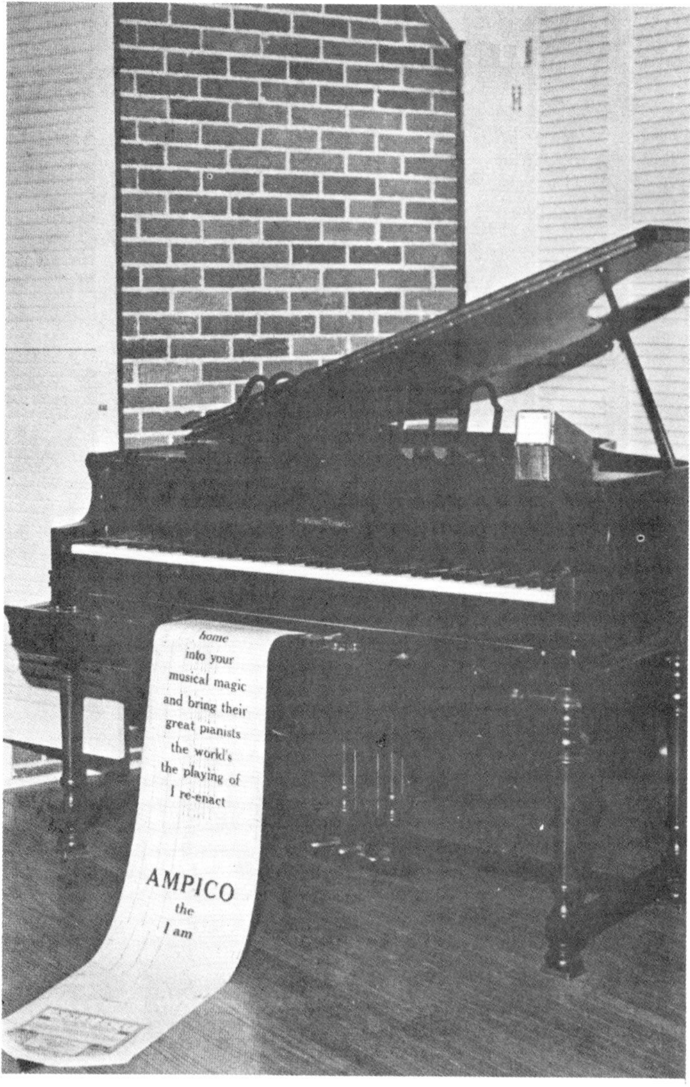

Fig. 10 - AMPICO Reproducing Piano

One of the least desirable features of all player pianos was the music roll drive motor. This was usually an air-motor consisting of bellows connected to a crankshaft. When the piano played loudly the motor was the least efficient. Just when the piano mechanism needed its maximum suction, much of it had to be diverted to make the music roll move. Hickman suggested an electric roll drive system, which was later incorporated into the Model B Ampico. This enabled the piano rolls to be of any length, and Ampico issued a series of long playing rolls with the B model. Some of these ran for nearly half an hour.[10]

One of the most important inventions was the development of the variable-bleed valve unit, developed by Hickman in 1925. The unit valves controlled the stack of striker pneumatics, which did the actual playing and were located under the forward part of the sounding board of the piano. The striker pneumatics actuated the keys by lifting the rear ends from the underside. The double-valve system, in use on the Model A, was replaced by a single valve unit, developed by Hickman. The change in the valve construction eliminated the noise of one set of valves completely, and otherwise reduced the noise from the valve action to a point where it could not possibly be heard. The single valve unit, which was much less costly, and more efficient than the double unit, also made it possible to do away with the outside valve unit that hung down so low on the Model A.[11] (Fig. 11)

In 1927, Hickman invented a device that was featured in the Model B piano, eliminating a problem found in almost all player pianos. After a roll had played, it would rewind. However, it was then necessary to rewind the rolls by hand, as they never rewound tightly enough. Hickman devised a brake drum mounted on the axle of the takeup spool. At intervals a mechanism would actuate the brake, which would stop the rotation of the take up spool momentarily, and the continued motion of the music roll spool would tighten the paper. A clutch in the axle prevented accidental lockup and damage to the motor.[12]

The last piano improvement for which Hickman is credited was the automatic tracking system featured on the Model B Ampico. Most player pianos were built with systems that could handle only one size roll. Music rolls were usually made from unglazed paper, which picked up moisture, and would alternately expand and contract, necessitating manual adjustment of the mechanism. Hickman devised a tracking system which:

> ...consisted of a rod with a metal tracker tip on each end suspended between two springs attached to brass leaves which lightly rested on the edges of the music roll. This mechanism could compensate for various widths of music rolls, and could maintain a centering accuracy to within five thousands of an inch.[13]

VALVE UNIT

Filed June 4, 1927

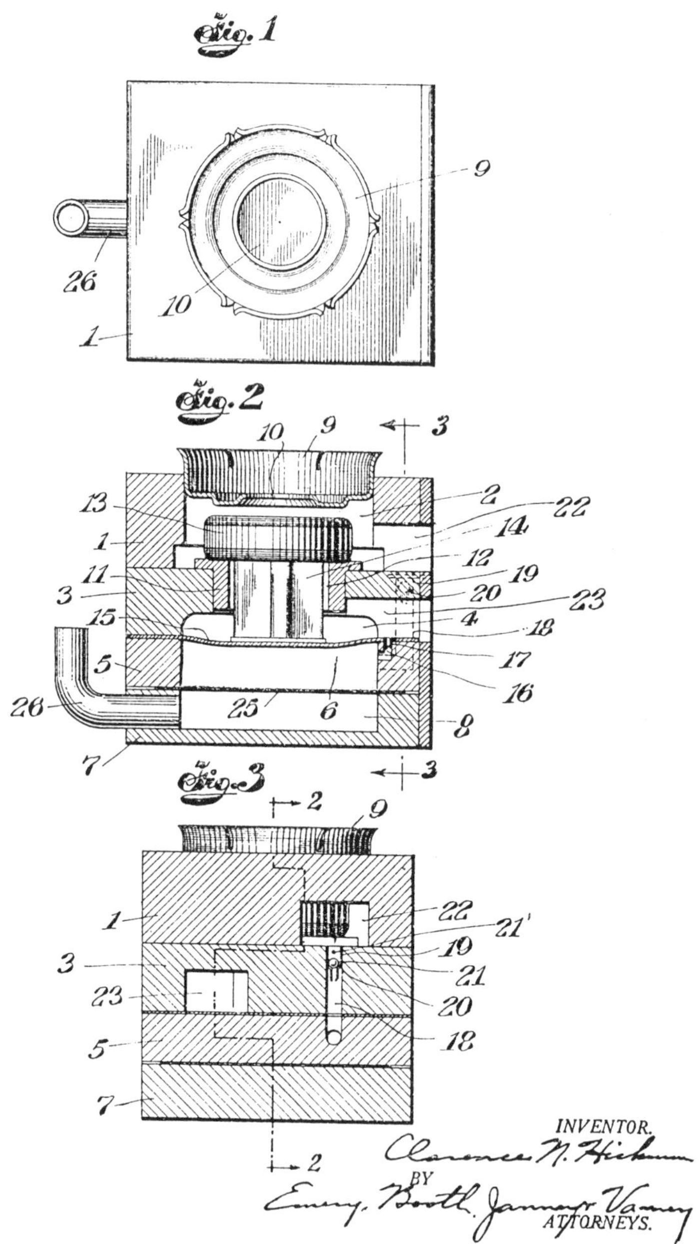

Fig. 11

It is interesting to note, with all of the above developments, that only the ball valve unit is patented in Hickman's name. He holds two other patents, one for piano key action and one for grand piano action, neither of which deals with reproducing pianos. In his tribute to Charles Stoddard, Director of the Research Laboratories, Hickman wrote of a meeting between the two of them, during which Stoddard conveyed concern about Hickman's many piano improvements:

> He said I had contributed so much to the development of the Model B Ampico that if the patents were issued in my name the officials would want to know what he had been doing. I told him that it was he who had the idea of getting a technical man and that it was his vision that had enabled me to make so many suggestions.[14]

Although the patents were then issued in Stoddard's name, he was so impressed that he helped Hickman gain an increase in salary from $7,500 per year to $10,000 per year, and it was made retroactive for one year.[15]

While at the piano company, Hickman performed many archery experiments, which will be covered later, but he also utilized the spark chronograph to do some research on golf. He measured the velocity of the club head and ball for many professional golfers, including Walter Hagen. The pros recommended that the golfer follow through, with the rationale that one could increase the velocity of the ball by pushing the ball after contact had been made. Hickman knew this could not be done, but carefully analyzed the spark chronograph readings. He found that when a golfer attempted to follow through, the maximum velocity of the club head was nearer the ball. So, although they could not affect velocity after the ball was hit, attempting to follow through caused the golfer to obtain a greater velocity of the clubhead prior to contacting the ball. This was one of the first attempts to scientifically prove a teaching cue or method.[16]

In 1929 the American Piano Company was sold to The Bankers Trust Company. After the stock market crash, the company went into the hands of receivers, and the Research Laboratory was closed on January 1, 1930. Immediately after, Hickman was able to get a position with the Bell Telephone Laboratories at West Street in New York.[17]

For the next twenty years, from 1930-1950, Hickman was to work in both the Acoustical and Switching Departments of Bell Laboratories. During that time, World War II intervened. Hickman continued to be employed by the Bell Labs, but during the peak of the war effort, he spent six of seven days on National Defense Committee work, again working with rocketry. During this span of 20 years, Hickman was granted 31 telephone and 37 rocket patents. Although each of these patents deals with noteworthy achievements in their respective fields, this book will mention selected ones, which best illustrate Hickman's ideas and mechanical genius.

Hickman's first assignment at the Bell Laboratories was to work with magnetic recording. Previous attempts had been made using magnetized steel wire. The large amounts of background noise, the noise of high speed wire movement, and the inability to record a wide range of sounds made the machine inefficient for practical use. Bell Labs felt that better devices could be developed and asked Hickman to spend his time in this area.[18] Within a year, Hickman had patented a new and improved magnetic tape recorder, then called a telegraphone. The basic changes consisted of different placements of the pole pieces or magnetized heads, an 1/8 inch flat tape rather than piano wire and a reduction in the speed of the tape from as much as six to eight feet per second to approximately one foot per second. This substantially reduced background noise and improved the quality of the reproduced sound.[19] (Fig. 12)

Hickman continued to improve his original version of the machine,

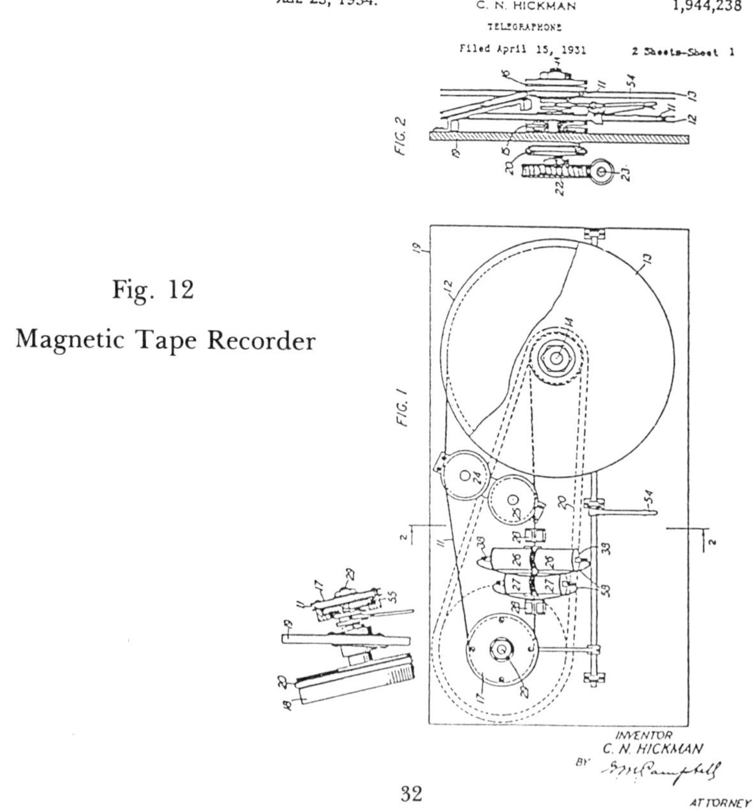

Fig. 12

Magnetic Tape Recorder

and the process was utilized by Bell Telephone at the 1939 New York World's Fair, among other places. At the exhibit called the "Audition for Visitors," members of the audience chosen at random were recorded talking with an interviewer. Moments later all the voices were played back in stereo sound so the entire audience could hear. The equipment was in operation thirteen hours a day seven days a week for the twenty-nine weeks of the World's Fair. About 110,000 people took part in the actual auditions, while many times that number enjoyed the demonstrations. Prior to this time high quality voice tape reproduction was unknown to the general public.[20] (Fig. 13)

In 1941, Hickman's improved recorder was made available to the general public under the name Mirrorphone. It was portable and was advertised as an excellent tool for instructors of voice training and public speaking, as the students could record and hear themselves instantly. An

Fig. 13   "Audition for Visitors" New York World's Fair 1939

Fig. 14

The Mirror Phone -- Magnetic Sound Recorder And Reproducer

experimental model was installed at the Julliard School of Music in New York, and advertisements were sent to schools as an aid in teaching foreign languages.[21] (Fig. 14)

In 1932 and again in 1937, Hickman received patents for a new device called a Telephone Message Recording System. Essentially this was the forerunner of the modern-day phone-answering machine. The apparatus involved a recording and reproducing unit plus the necessary switching mechanisms so that an incoming call could be recorded and later played back. The machine also had the capability of storing a message and playing it to an incoming caller.[22] One of the first uses of this machine was Bell's installation of a Weather-Announcing Tape Machine at its West Street office. A caller would dial a particular number and receive a recorded and updated weather report. This machine was installed in 1939 in New York City, and later in most large cities. The New York branch answered as many as 268,000 calls a day.[23] (Fig.15)

Hickman wrote an article in 1934 about a measuring instrument developed in his lab. A spectrometer is an instrument used to separate any kind of light into its different colors or wave lengths. The Bell Labs designed an Acoustic Spectrometer capable of separating complex sounds into their different components and at the same time indicating their approximate amplitudes. Prior to this device, the components had to be isolated one at a time. This new instrument enabled researchers to see all components of a sound instantly. The device provided a needed tool for

TELEPHONE MESSAGE RECORDING SYSTEM

Filed March 31, 1932   2 Sheets—Sheet 1

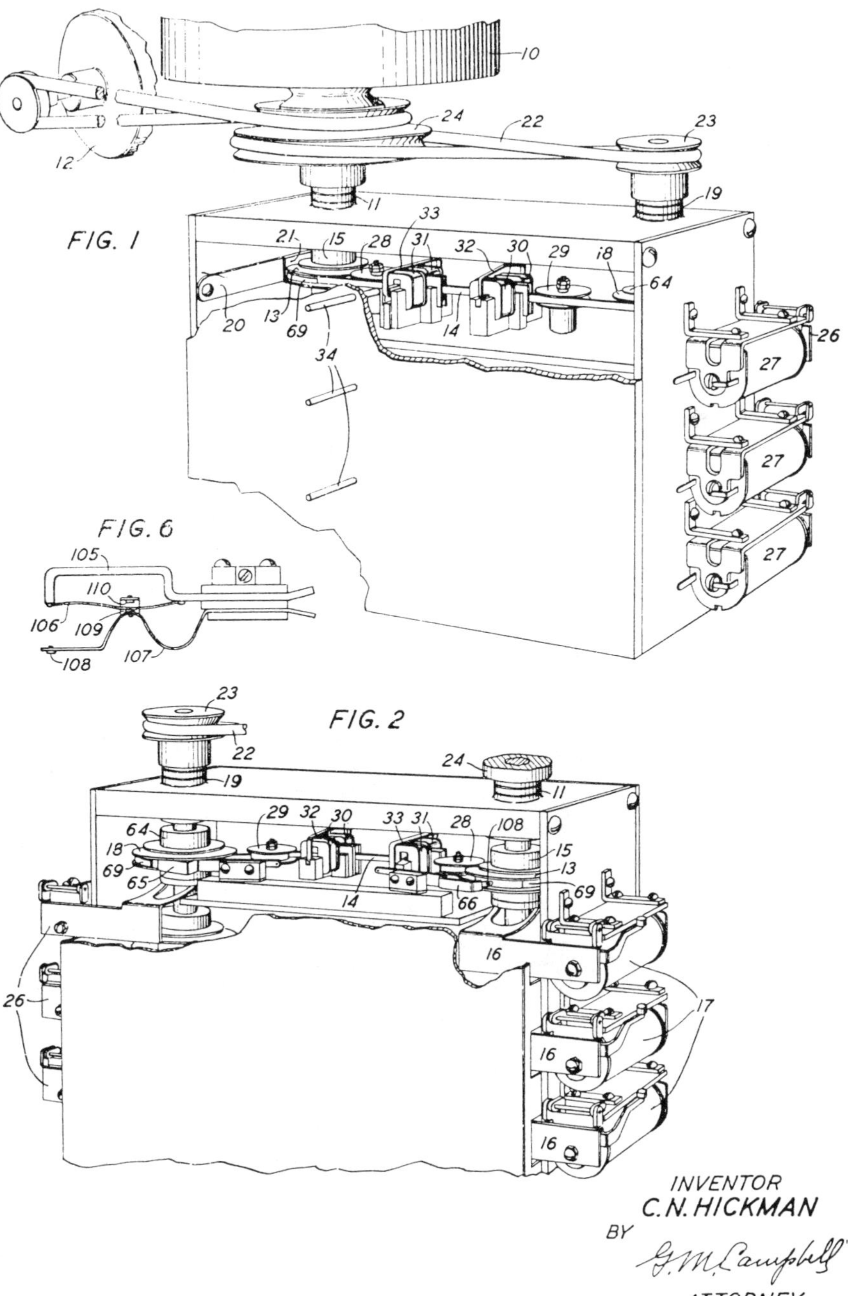

INVENTOR
C. N. HICKMAN
BY
G. M. Campbell
ATTORNEY

Fig. 15

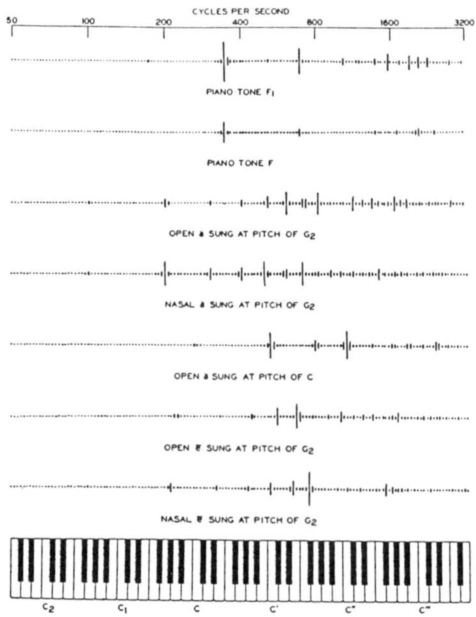

Fig. 16 Acoustic Spectogram

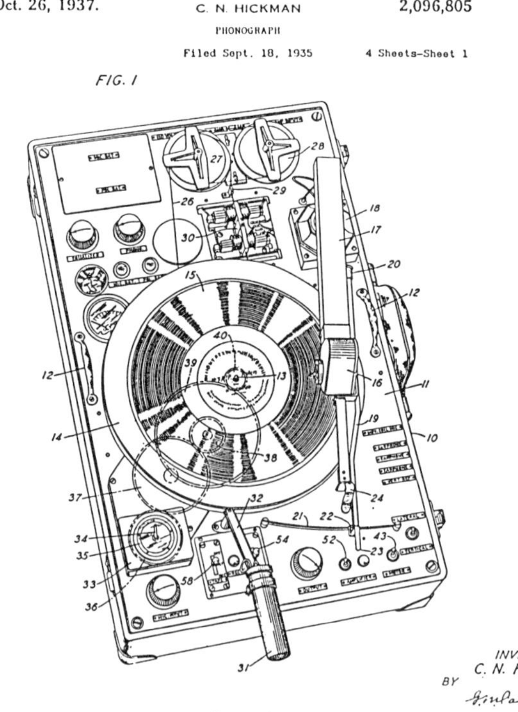

Fig. 17

studying the frequency components of sound of all types with results obtained almost instantly.[24] (Fig. 16)

The next year Hickman filed a patent for a device he called simply a "Phonograph." The uniqueness of this machine was that it served two purposes. It had a standard phonograph mechanism on top, capable of accepting a record disc. Inside the machine, however, was a tape recorder, capable of recording speech. It was Hickman's intention that the combined disc and telegraphone phonograph ". . . provides a convenient and compact device for aiding one in improving one's speech, and for home instruction in foreign languages."[25] (Fig. 17)

Before Hickman left the Acoustical Department at Bell Labs, he had at least ten patents in his name for various aspects of magnetic recording. In 1937, he was transferred to the Switching and Relay Department. This area dealt with magnetic, line, and multicontact relays for the telephones, as well as with various switches and connecting devices for telephone transmission. From 1940 to 1950, Hickman acquired 20 more patents dealing with relays and switches.

The 20 patents plus other devices not patented were worked on during a ten year span, five of which were spent working mostly for the government. As outlined in Chapter I, Hickman's foresight[26] led to the development of rockets for use during World War II, and he was put in charge of rocket development for the United States. His position was Chief of Section H (for Hickman), a division of the National Defense Research Committee. Hickman would ultimately receive 37 patents as a result of his war efforts. A selected group of his contributions will be mentioned here.

When Hickman first started his work for the government, he worked in a lab at the Dahlgreen Proving Grounds in Washington, D.C. As that area grew too crowded with different research labs, Hickman's group relocated to the Old Bombproof at the Naval Powder Factory, Indian Head Proving Ground, Maryland. A final relocation to the Allegheny Ballistics Laboratory in Cumberland, Maryland provided the necessary room for rocket developments. Hickman also coordinated a lab at California Technological Institute and travelled back and forth between the labs when necessary.[27]

One of the first tasks assigned to Hickman's group was to produce a jet-accelerated armour piercing bomb. The first ideas for the bomb had originated with Goddard and Hickman in their early experiments during World War I. The Navy exhibited interest in this project, and Section H developed the necessary bomb. It was first flight tested on November 27, 1941, but was not successful, as it did not ignite. On June 4, 1942, one bomb ignited at 1,000 feet and accelerated, but the other did not ignite.

Hickman, seeing the ignition problems all along, had come up with another idea and had Bell Labs working on it for him. The fourteen-inch bomb had used a clock-driven fuse. Hickman's system was activated after a measured distance of fall, using the rotation of four propeller blades as a guage to trigger ignition. This was named the H-1 fuse. The Navy

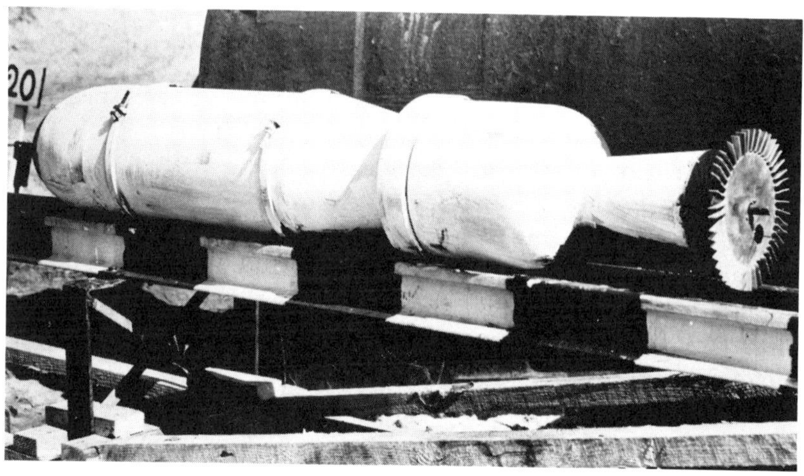

Fig. 18   14 Inch Jet Propelled Armour Piercing Bomb

decided to apply the principle of jet acceleration to the existing twelve-inch armour piercing bomb and phased out the production of the fourteen-inch bomb. Although it required much re-design, the twelve-inch bomb was developed utilizing Hickman's ignition system, and all subsequent testing proceeded without incident. The bombs were accelerated from 185 to 205 feet per second, depending upon weight. This particular bomb was never highly developed for use during the war.[28] As a result of the initial project, Section H was thrust into a frenzy developing numerous rockets for various uses.

Hickman had developed the recoilless rifle during World War I while working for Goddard, but production of the rifle never materialized due to lack of funding after the end of the war. One of the first things Hickman did was reactivate the design for the recoilless rifle, later known as the Bazooka. The Bazooka was given its name by General Thomas J. Hayes. During a demonstration of the weapon in June 1942, the General compared it to the "Bazooka," a stage prop used by Bob Burns, a comedian of the time.[29] The purpose of the Bazooka was to project a rocket which weighed about three pounds and was amazingly effective against armour. The Bazooka had little recoil since it used a self-propelled 2.36 inch projectile which was loaded by one soldier and fired by another. It was well known for its effectiveness against tanks. The Bazooka rockets themselves did not really penetrate armour, but punched a hole through thick steel plate by a directed and concentrated blast that threw hot fragments of steel around inside the tanks. In some cases, the rockets blasted as much as six inches of armour plate. The Bazooka was first used in the North Africa landings in November 1942, and was enthusiastically used by the foot soldiers of Patton's army. A later model of the Bazooka, developed by 1944, called the Super Bazooka, was able to penetrate fourteen inches of armour plate.[30] (Fig. 19,20,21,22,23)

Not every one of Hickman's developments was as spectacular as the Bazooka, but they were nevertheless valuable. One of the functions of Hickman's laboratory was to make both internal and external ballistic measurements. The internal measurements consisted of making, among other things, gas pressure and rocket thrust measurements. In the early tests on rockets, commercial copper and lead cylindrical pressure gauges were used. These gauges had been developed for measuring the peak pressure in guns. This particular gauge simply would not give the required pressure range for the rocket analysis. Hickman suggested replacing the cylinders with copper balls, and asked Bell Labs to produce and anneal (a heating and cooling process used for softening and making

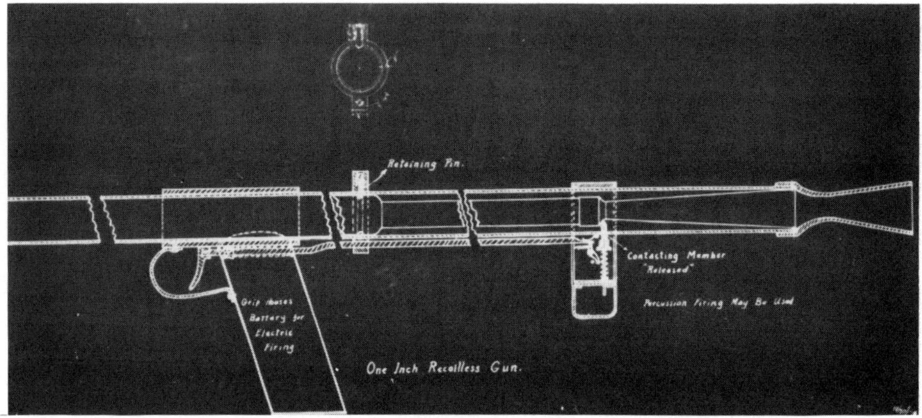

Fig. 19

Reproduction from lantern slide of drawing made by C.N. Hickman in October 1918 at Pasadena, California while working for Dr. Goddard. The original drawing with Hickman's initials and date was given to the Aeronautical Institute in New York City for display purposes along with many other Goddard items. The gun was demonstrated at Aberdeen in the Fall of 1918.

elements less brittle)[31] the required balls for the gauges. Gas pressures ranging from 300 to 10,000 pounds per square inch could be determined by using these balls. About 4 million of the copper balls were produced during World War II.[32] The use of the copper balls instead of cylinders for measuring the pressure in the explosion chambers of rockets and mortars not only proved of great value in ordnance studies but resulted in savings several times greater than the total amount the Bell Labs spent on all its rocket developments.[33] In a recent article, Dr. Ralph Gibson, Director Emeritus of the Johns Hopkins University Applied Physics Laboratory, reminisced on working in this particular area with Dr. Hickman:

> The chief instrument for measuring the pressure developed in a rocket motor had up till then been an adaptation of the "crusher gauge" universally used in guns. A steel ball held between the base of a steel cylinder and the face of a moveable piston was deformed by the pressure of the surrounding gases on the piston, and the amount of deformation as measured by calipers was correlated with the maximum pressure to which the gauge was exposed. Dr. Hickman used balls of annealed copper instead of steel in order to provide a better measure of the maximum pressure in rockets which was far less than that in guns. The use of this device earned for him a nickname with anatomical undertones in the rocket fraternity.[34] (Fig. 24)

Besides the problems of making internal measurements, Hickman's lab was also confronted with the formidable problem, for that time, of making external ballistic measurements. It was necessary to measure such things as the behavior of the jet, yaw, velocity, acceleration, burning time, burning distance, range, and dispersion. Methods for measuring the velocity of shells fired from guns were not applicable to the rocket program because the burning of the rocket continued through from 50 to 1,000 feet of travel through the air. No spark chronograph or known method of measuring shell velocities could be used. Early on, Hickman used a high-speed camera of his own which he designed and built to try to follow the rocket through all its trajectory, but it was still a tremendous task to measure the film and interpret the measurements. Hickman recognized the tremendous need for a single camera that would follow the rocket through the entire trajectory in which burning took place. He reasoned that since the flight path of the rocket was well known, the width or height of the picture did not have to be very great. He calculated that a quarter-inch height was adequate to take care of any dispersion that might be expected in the rocket's flight. He also sought to develop a camera that was portable and light in weight. Hickman, utilizing his

Fig. 20   Rocket fired from original recoilless rifle at Aberdeen Proving Grounds in 1918.

Fig. 21   Original Bazooka Being Fired By Officer (May 1942)

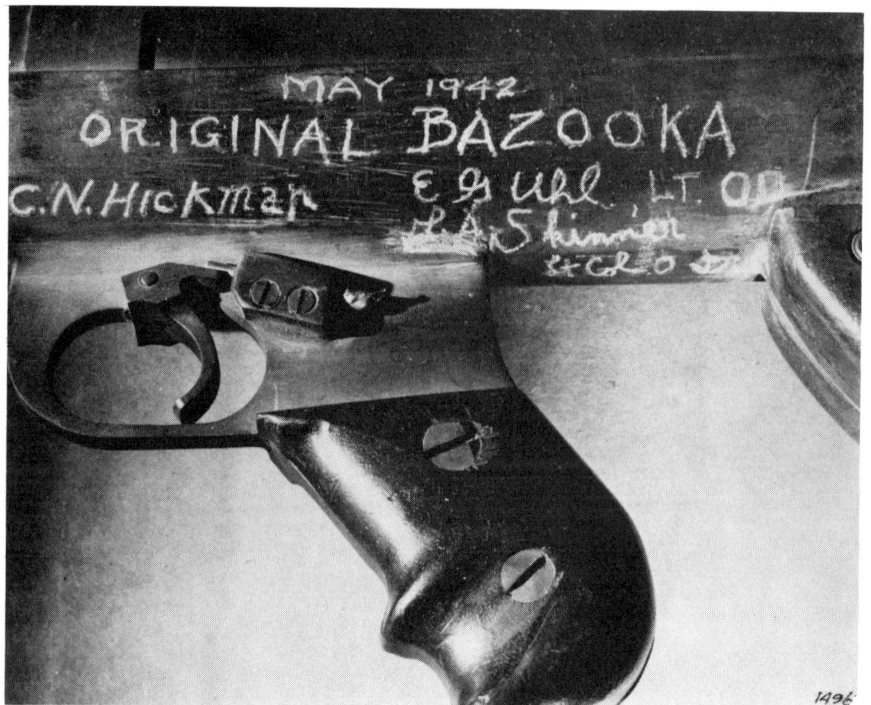

Fig. 22

The original, autographed model of the Bazooka is in the museum at West Point.

knowledge of photography, took on the task of designing such a camera, which he called the Ribbon Frame camera. In a move that was indicative of the high regard in which Bell Labs held his abilities, the Labs consented to build one of the cameras without drawings, which would have been very time consuming. Hickman worked with Frank Reck of the Special Apparatus Department at Bell Labs, and the Ribbon Frame camera was built under Hickman's step-by-step directions. The National Defense Research Committee realized the value of the tool and quickly had six more cameras produced. It is possible to see, in the accompanying photographs, the invaluable tool that Hickman created for the study of rockets at the time. (Fig. 25,26,27,28)

Another tool devised by Hickman for measurement purposes was the Rocket Spinner. Rockets were ordinarily stabilized by fins, but a variety of circumstances caused them to lose stability and alignment. Such conditions were common with very high-speed rockets where the

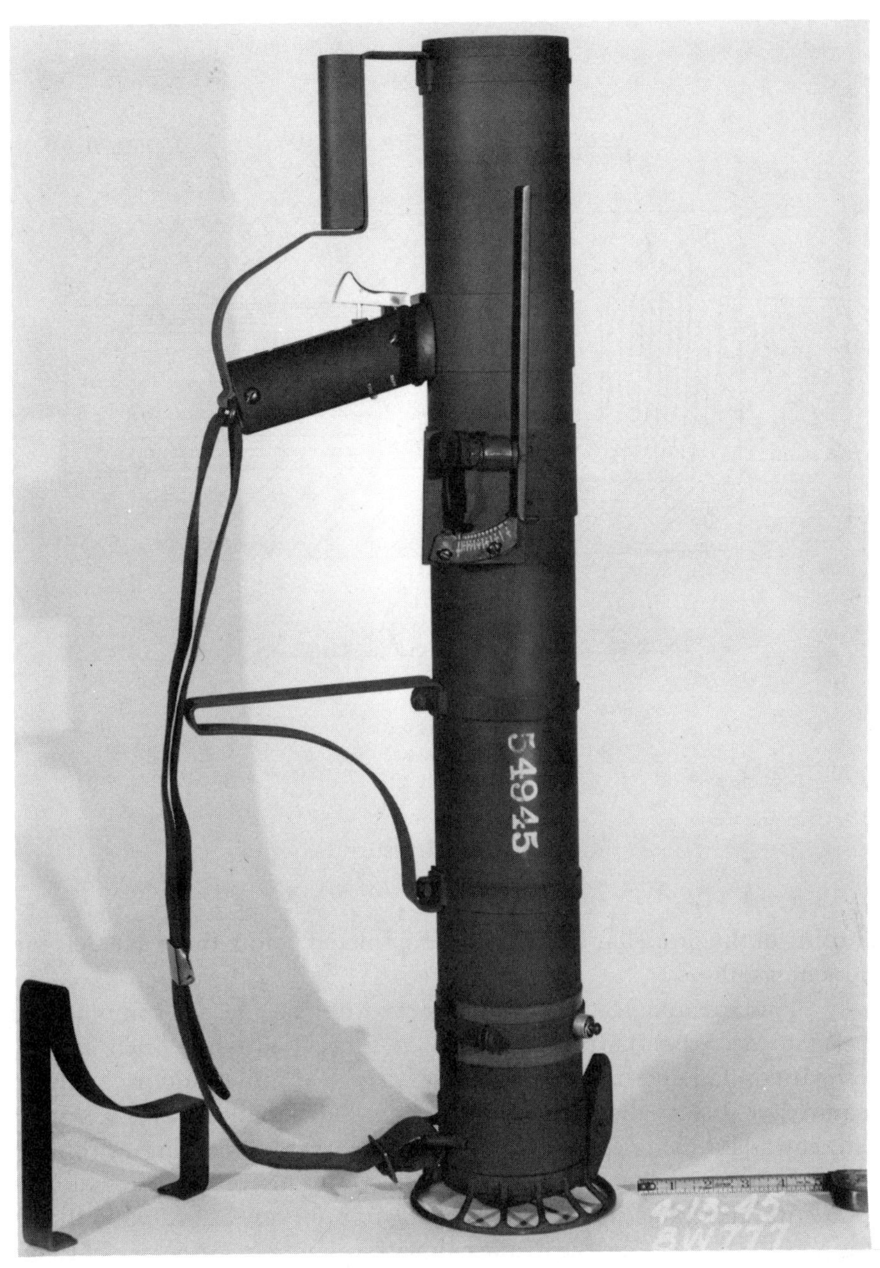

Fig. 23

The Super Bazooka Launching Tube, capable of firing rockets
which could pierce 14" of armour.

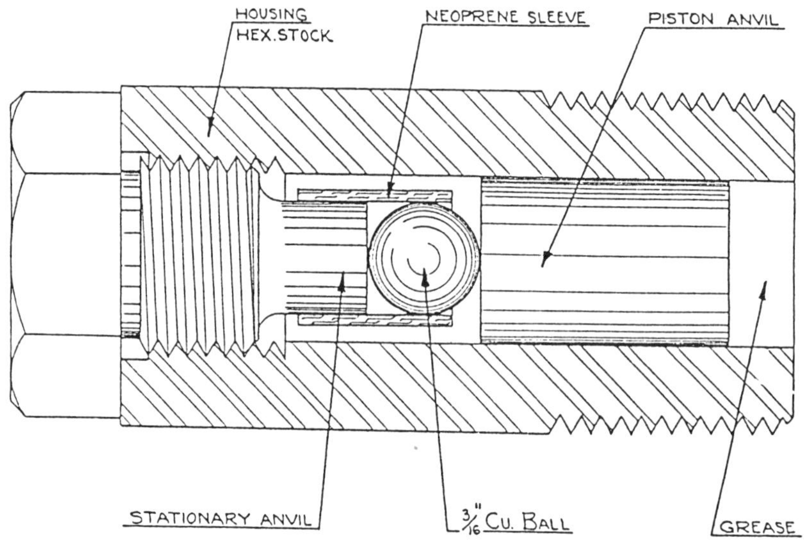

Fig. 24

Copper Ball Pressure Gauge

burning of the propellant couldn't be completed before the rocket left the launching tube.

Goddard and Hickman had worked on the idea of spinning the rocket to decrease the dispersion under such conditions, but early investigations had determined that a high degree of spin would probably be required to bring about an improvement. Hickman devised a system whereby a launching tube was mounted on large ball bearings within an outer stationary tube attached to a tripod. A motor was provided to rotate the launching tube at speeds of 900 to 2700 rps. It was found that it was possible to decrease the dispersion with very moderate spins. Without spin, the dispersion for the standard rocket would be a deviation of about 39 feet for 1000 feet of travel, while spins of 800, 1400, and 2400 rps would decrease the deviation. The improvement in dispersion obtained in tests using this device resulted in intensive research programs to reduce

Fig. 25

Ribbon Frame Camera (Frank Reck)

Fig. 26

Ribbon Frame Camera Open Without Film

Fig. 27

A 4 ½ inch rocket being fired from a plane. Velocity of the plane is about 350 feet per second. Velocity of the rocket is about 900 feet per second. Velocity of the rocket relative to the earth is therefore 1250 feet per second.

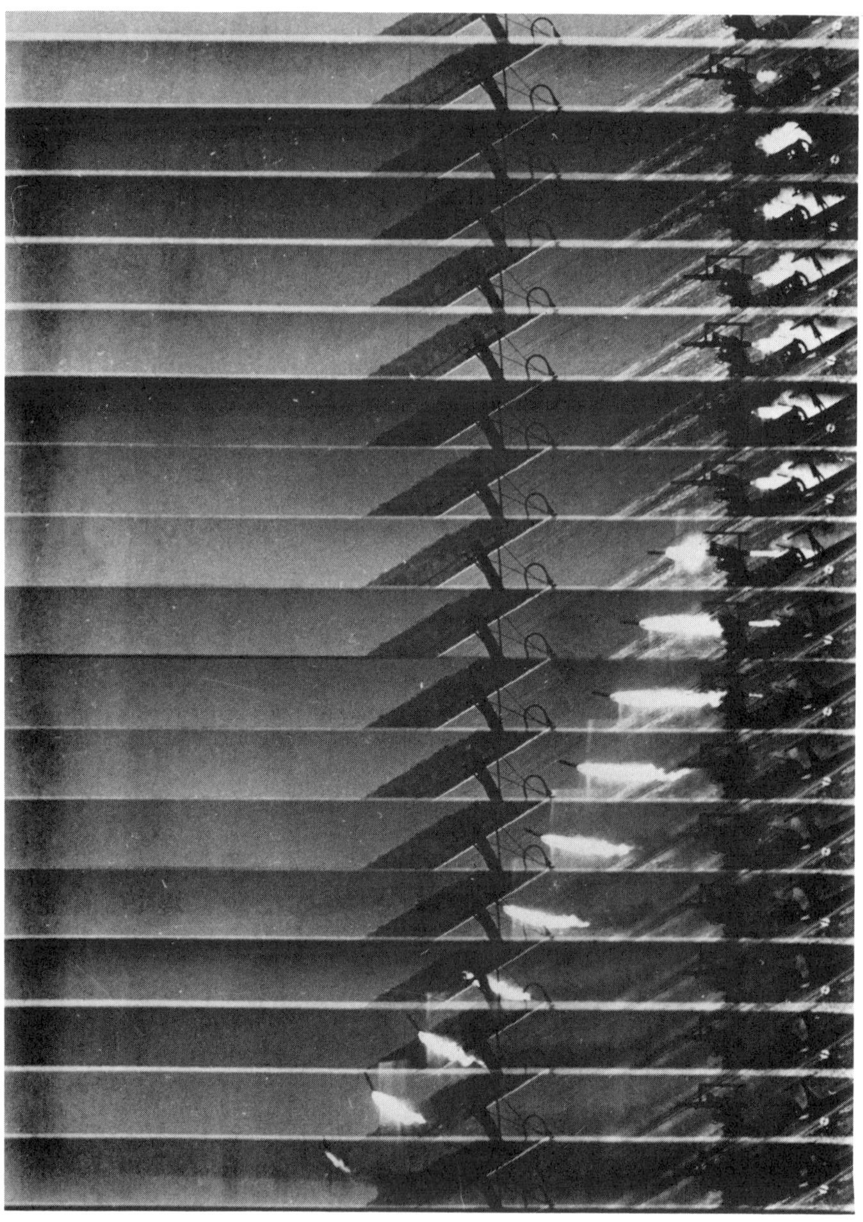

Fig. 28

4½ inch rocket with large dispersion due to malalignment with center of gravity.

dispersions by giving the rocket a moderate spin at the time of launching.[36]

The devices developed by Hickman and his lab were very extensive and highly technical. Each was keenly important to the development of rocketry. Although not all will be mentioned, three should not be omitted. The 4½ inch rocket with folding stabilizer fins was an important innovation. It could be fired from planes, tanks, and special vehicles (multiple launchers), as well as from the portable launcher shown in accompanying photographs. (Fig. 29,30,31,32)

Fig. 29

4½ Inch Rocket Leaving The Spinning Launcher

The rocket driver was an ingenious device used with the recoilless 4.2 inch gun. Normally, when the gun barrel was placed at an angle, a shell dropped in the tube was forced by gravity against the percussion cap. However, when the gun was in a horizontal position, the rocket driver was attached to the shell, the firing pin pulled, and the rockets drove the shell against the firing pin. (See photographs) After firing, the rocket fell away.

The last to be mentioned, and the use which Hickman so clearly foresaw in 1918, was the use of rockets on airplanes. Hickman devised the rockets, the methods of mounting, and the delayed firing mechanism necessary for the successful use of air rockets.[37]

Fig. 30 4½ inch Rocket with Folding Fin stabilized

Hickman's foresight and mechanical genius, with its application to the development of the necessary apparatus and tools, was directly responsible for American jet-propulsion, almost non-existent at the beginning of the war, becoming one of the important factors in the war victory. For his exceptional service during the war effort, Hickman was given the highest award bestowed upon a civilian, The Medal of Merit. The medal was presented by Admiral Kinkaid, February 2, 1948, at the White House. (See Appendix D and E) (Fig. 35)

Hickman's inventive genius was not restricted to his varied occupational fields, for his accomplishments with his hobbies were noteworthy. The physicist's mind was always at work while he seriously pursued his two favorite activities, magic and archery.

Were it not for the rocket accident that caused him to lose part of his fingers, Hickman probably would have become a professional magician. He became interested in magic when he was six years old and went on two tours in 1911 and 1912 as The Hoosier Magician. All the illusions and tricks he performed were of his own creation. He was an honored member of the International Brotherhood of Magicians and the American Society of Magicians in Washington, D.C. His most famous trick, described below, was recorded by the Society as an original magic trick. His accident never stopped his performing, and he gave magic

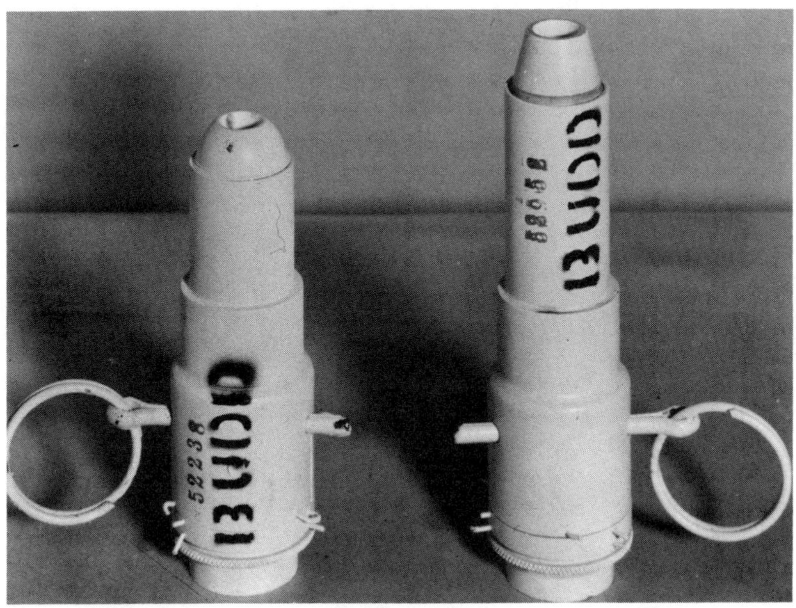

Fig. 31 Driver rockets for the 4.2 inch recoilless mortar

Fig. 32　4.2 Inch Recoilless Gun being fired in a horizontal position.
The Driver Rocket drives the shell against the firing pin.

Fig. 33 Plane in flight carrying 20 - 115mm rockets

Fig. 34   115 MM Rockets Under Wing of Plane

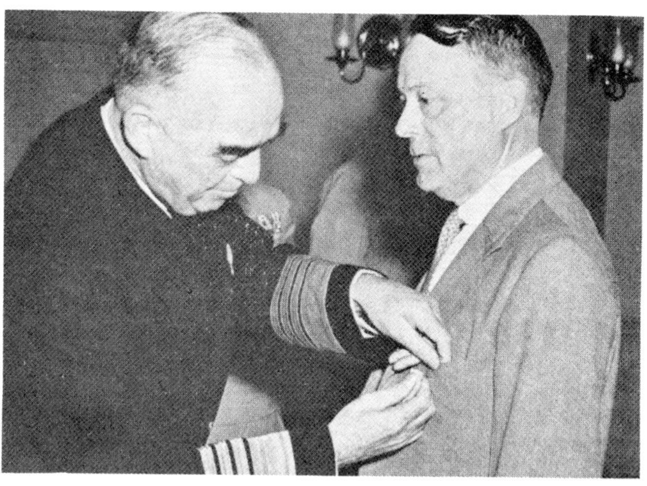

Fig. 35 Admiral Thomas C. Kinkaid presents Medal for Merit to C.N. Hickman for his leadership in the development of rockets during World War II.

demonstrations at many social and professional functions until his death. He published one article and gave many speeches on magic.[39] During World War II his main relaxation was meeting with the American Society of Magicians once each month. During each of these meetings he would present one original magic trick, and he became known as their "Science Member." His most outstanding trick, which could not be analyzed by either magicians' society, was technically excellent. The following is his description of the trick as presented to the Society of American Magicians at the National Press Club in Washington, D.C. during the War:

One evening I showed up with a plastic board that had a pocket on one side large enough to hold a deck of cards and another pocket on the other side large enough to take one card. The plastic board had a handle. I then gave a member of the audience a deck of cards and had him go into the audience and let ten or twelve people select any card, look at it and then hold it between their palms. I then had another member take the deck and go out and let them push their card into the deck. I then took this deck and would put one card at a time into the front pocket and I would tell them if it was one of the cards that had been held by one of the members. After doing this for a few times I told them that I would tell them how it was done. I told them that I had in-

vented an olfactory amplifier and that the scent picked up from
the palms of their hands was amplified and that it touched off a
breakdown tube causing a lamp to light and all I had to do was to
see if the lamp lighted. I then took a hood off a bulb inside the
plastic board and continued the examination of the cards.
Whenever I came to a card that had been held, the lamp would
light and they could see it. Well, I pulled their leg a little more by
telling them that I had developed my sense of smell so that I could
pick out the card by smell. I then continued the examination of
the cards and when I came to one that had been held I would
predict this and as soon as I put it in the little pocket the lamp
would light up.[40]

Hickman had the showmanship, sense of humor, and technical
knowledge to have become a superb magician, but he never pursued the
field seriously due to the loss of his fingers. Such was not the case with his
other hobby. He overcame his physical handicap and utilized his tremendous technical background to enjoy and contribute immeasureably to the
sport of archery.

REFERENCES

1. Clarence N. Hickman, "Alternating-Current Resistance and Inductance of
   Single-Layer Coils," *Scientific Papers of the Bureau of Standards*
   472, (Washington, D.C.: Government Printing Office, May 3, 1923),
   Hickman Archives

2. Clarence N. Hickman, "A Variable Resistor of Low Value," *Journal of the
   Optical Society of America and Review of Scientific Instruments*, 6
   (October 1922): 848-51.

3. Clarence N. Hickman, "Highlights in the Life of Clarence N. Hickman,"
   October 15, 1980, p.9, Hickman Archives.

4. *Ibid.*

5. Clarence N. Hickman, "Submarine Mine," Patent #2,439,211,
   United States Patent Office, Washington, D.C. Filed
   November 13, 1924, Granted April 6, 1948, Hickman Archives.

6. Larry Givens, *Re-enacting the Artist*, (New York: Vestal Press, 1970), p.8.

7 .Ibid., p.25.

8 .Clarence N. Hickman, "Spark Chronograph Developed for Measuring
   Intensity of Percussion Instrument Tones," *Acoustical Journal*,
   (October 1929): 138-46. Hickman Archives.

9. Givens, *Re-enacting the Artist*, pp. 35-41.

10. *Ibid.*, p.60

11. Ampico Corporation, *Service Manual*, (New York: Ampico, 1929), pp. 3,4 and Givens, *Re-enacting the Artist*, pp. 61,66.

12. Givens, *Re-enacting the Artist*, p. 67 and Ampico Corporation, *Service Manual*, p.46.

13. Givens, *Re-enacting the Artist*, p.70.

14. Clarence N. Hickman, "A Tribute to Charles Fuller Stoddard, Inventor of the Ampico Reproducing Piano, and Director of The American Piano Company Research Laboratory." (Original full draft of a speech given to the Automatic Musical Instrument Collectors Association Convention, Philadelphia, June 30, 1979), Hickman Archives.

15. *Ibid.*

16. Hickman, "Hightlights," p.8.

17. Hickman, "A Tribute to Charles Fuller Stoddard..."

18. Hickman, "Highlights," p.6.

19. Clarence N. Hickman, "Telegraphone," Patent #1,944,238, United States Patent Office, Washington, D.C. Filed April 15, 1931, Granted January 23, 1934. Hickman Archives.

20. "The Bell System at the New York World's Fair," *Bell Laboratories Record*, (September 1939), and R.A. Cushman, "Audition Demonstration," *Bell Laboratories Record* (May 1940):273-77 Hickman Archives.

21. "The Mirrorphone," *Bell Laboratories Record*, 20 (September 1941):2-5.

22. Clarence N. Hickman, "Telephone Message Recording System," Patent #2,006,455 United States Patent Office, Washington, D.C. Filed March 31, 1932, Granted July 2, 1935. Hickman Archives.

23. R.A. Cushman, "Weather Announcing Tape Machine," *Bell Laboratories Record* (November 1939):70-71, and "Retirements," *Bell Laboratories Record*, (January 1950):38-39. Hickman Archives.

24. Clarence N. Hickman, "Acoustic Spectrometer," *Bell Laboratories Record*, 12 (October 1934):60-62.

25. Clarence N. Hickman, "Phonograph," Patent #2,096,805 United States Patent Office, Washington, D.C., Filed September 18, 1935, Granted October 26, 1937. Hickman Archives.

26. Clarence N. Hickman, Letter to Dr. F.B. Jewett, President of National Academy of Sciences and Bell Telephone, "An Investigation Pertaining to Rockets," June 20, 1940, and F.B. Jewett, Letter to Major General C.M. Wesson, Chief of Ordnance, Washington, C.D., June 20, 1940, Hickman Archives.

27. Clarence N. Hickman, *Genealogy of the Hickman Families of Virginia, Kentucky, Indiana and Texas,* (Jackson Heights, N.Y.: Westminster Printing Company, 1967), p.52.

28. Dr. Loren Morey, *The Powder Rockets (1917-1942) -- A History of Solid Fuel Rocket Development*, (Copy of original manuscript), p.VIIIA 6-7, Hickman Archives.

29. *Ibid.*, P.VIID - 14.

30. Clarence N. Hickman, "Problems and Accomplishments on Contract
    OEMsr-256," Memorandum for File, November 2, 1943,
    Hickman Archives.

31. Clarence N. Hickman, "Ballistic Measurements and Performance of
    Rockets," A talk given by Hickman at a preliminary exhibition and
    demonstration for the renegotiation committee, July 6, 1945.
    Hickman Archives.

32. *Ibid.*

33. "Rocket Researcher," *Bell Telephone Magazine*, 23 (February 1945):37-39.

34. R.E. Gibson, "Personal Reflections on the Origins of the
    Chemical Propulsion Information Agency,"
    CPIA Bulletin, 7(October 1981):1-4.

35. Clarence N. Hickman, "Problems and Accomplishments..."; and
    Clarence N. Hickman, "Ballistic Measurements..."; and F.R. Reck,
    "The Ribbon-Frame Camera," *Bell Laboratories Record*,
    23(February 1945):40-45.

36. Clarence N. Hickman, "Problems and Accomplishments..."; and
    "Rocket Researcher," *Bell Laboratories Record*, p.38; and
    Clarence N. Hickman, "Ballistic Measurement and Performance...";
    and "Rocket Spinner," *Bell Laboratories Record*,
    24(May 1946):183-84.

37. Dr. Loren Morey, *The Powder Rockets*, p.VIID-4; Gladeon M. Barnes,
    Weapons of World War II, (New York: D.Van Nostrand., 1947); and
    F.B. Jewett, Letter to Major General C.M. Wesson, Chief of Ordance,
    Washington, D.C. June 4, 1940. Hickman Archives.

38. *Bell Laboratories Record*, Vol. 26 (August 1948,) p. 345.
    Hickman Archives.

39. Clarence N. Hickman, "There is No Such Thing As a New Card Trick,"
    M.U.M., 55 (June 1965), and Clarence N. Hickman,
    "A New Technique for Making Objects Invisible," Presentation before
    the Society of American Magicians, Washington Assembly No. 23,
    June 13, 44, Hickman Archives.

40. Clarence N. Hickman, Letter to Dr. Harvey Fletcher, February 3, 1945,
    p. 9, Hickman Archives.

Fig. 36 Clarence N. Hickman, 6 golds at 30 yards, 1946

CHAPTER

III

FROM THE ART OF ARCHERY
TO THE SCIENCE OF ARCHERY

Hickman was uniquely qualified, because of his outstanding technical background, to contribute in precedent-setting ways to his favorite sport, archery. Although he pursued it as a hobby and recreational activity, he approached it with the keen mind of the scientist. He spent over seventy years in this activity, actively participating, and seeking to increase the efficiency of the equipment with which he was working.

Hickman's interest in archery began in 1895, at the age of six, when he was taught to shoot by his father and brothers. His father had learned the art of making bows and arrows from Hickman's paternal grandfather, who had been taught by the Cherokee Indians of Kentucky. Since the early Hickmans were taught by Indians, they used the pinch draw (squeezing arrow and string between thumb and first finger), as opposed to the three-finger or English technique in use now (first three fingers on string, arrow fits between first and second finger, thumb is not used). They did not anchor on the draw (draw string to a stopping place on face), but pulled to about breast level with the bow held at a 45 degree angle. The aiming was completely instinctive.
The Indians also influenced the Hickmans' arrow design. The arrows had no feathers but were weighted at the point ends so they were stable.[1]

As Hickman and his brothers grew up, they all lost their interest in shooting. His father, who also had stopped shooting, renewed his interest in archery when he was 75 years old. A methodist minister had helped him become active in a small archery club, and he learned about the English method of shooting. He adopted the three-finger draw, which made it easier to draw a heavy bow.

Hickman's father visited him in New York City in 1924 and brought his bow. Hickman's old enthusiasm for the sport returned at once. He quickly made a bow like his father's, and they shot together in the Bronx woods. The bows his father used ranged in weight from 45 to 65 pounds (pounds of pressure required to pull the string a specific distance, usually 28 inches). Several years after that, about 1927, Hickman became ill, and, at the advice of his doctor who suggested an exercise program, he practiced archery on a regular basis. Due to his very light build (weight 117 lbs.) he was unable to pull the bow weights required to shoot successfully with the straight limb long bows of that time.[2]

Hickman's physical problem spurred his interest in beginning a scientific study of the bow to improve its efficiency so that he might perform better. He discovered several years later that he had a spot on his lungs, probably tuberculosis, that was responsible for his low weight and ill health. He continually attributed his health improvement to his involvement in archery, and the tale of his archery contributions begins at this point. The same year that his father had renewed his interest in shooting, Hickman had accepted a job in the research department of the American Piano Company in New York. He had access to a number of sources for research data and testing equipment from 1924 to 1929. Following his doctor's suggestion in 1927, he became seriously interested in archery, and in his leisure time, concentrated on the physics of bows and arrows in order to improve their efficiency.

Hickman's research in archery was simplified by the fact that the piano company had purchased an Aberdeen Chronograph from the Lees and Northrup Company for use in measuring the velocity of hammers. Hickman's desire to work on some of his experiments at home led him to design and construct a portable chronograph, capable of operating on AC as well as DC current.[3] Later, Hickman wrote to John P. Craven, Chief Scientist, Department of the Navy, in response to a request for information:

> I have the largest collection of books on archery privately owned in this country. Unfortunately they do not give much information on the ballistics of an arrow. Up until I made measurements in 1928, no one had ever measured the velocity of an arrow by any means other than a stop watch. I made use of a chronograph to measure the velocity and acceleration of arrows of different weights shot from bows of different designs.[4]

In January 1931, Hickman had an article published in the *Journal of the Franklin Institute* entitled "A Portable Spark Chronograph for Use on Either Direct or Alternating Current." A chronograph is an instrument for measuring the time of flight of projectiles.[5] Unlike the heavier Aberdeen Chronograph, Hickman's machine was portable, and could be

used on any voltage from 50-250.* As a direct result of having developed
the Spark Chronograph, Hickman began a series of scientific investigations that would shed light on the physics of bow and arrow design.
Although the article on the Spark Chronograph appeared only in 1931,
Hickman's scientific articles appeared somewhat earlier. Utilizing the
chronograph, he was able to provide data dealing with factors affecting
bow and arrow performance. (Fig. 37)

Fig. 37 Hickman Spark Chronograph

The chronograph made by Hickman was used for testing bows and
arrows until about 1940. When he was placed in charge of rocket
development during World War II, he used his chronograph to record
velocity of rockets in flight, prior to his invention of the ribbon frame
camera.[7]

Earl Hoyt, Jr., founder of Hoyt Archery Company, the world's
largest manufacturer of top tournament target archery bows, purchased
the Hickman Spark Chronograph in 1958 from Dr. Hickman for $300.

---

*Hickman's chronograph was capable of recording six events and had an accuracy of better than 1
percent. The speed of its motor was 2000 rpm. One revolution took .030 second. One-third revolution, which was the length of one measured segment, took .010 second.[6]

The machine was responsible for changes in bow design and matching of arrows to bows and added considerably to the technology in use today. Shortly after Hoyt's purchase, Hoyt reported some of his find-dings to Hickman:

> You will probably be interested in some of the results that we are getting. Bows in the 42 to 45 pound weight bracket (at 28 inch draw) are producing velocities with #1816 Easton Shafting of 190 to 200 feet per second, 170 to 179 feet per second for the one ounce arrow. Our testing is just beginning. We are experimenting with different core tapers, both single and compound--and various bow limb geometry. Also, present results seem to indicate that a working limb of approximately 19½ to 20 inches to be the most efficient for any bow length....Your spark chronograph has afforded me one of the greatest pleasures that I have had in some time. To obtain accurate results is a real thrill and of infinite value to us in evaluating the merits of various bow designs. I can-not express how glad I am that we were able to obtain the Hickman Spark Chronograph at this time. It is one of the best in-vestments I ever made.

In today's modern bow analysis, all new bows are subjected to modern chronographic tests, and the results of arrow speed in feet per second are noted in manufacturer's results. Theoretically, the faster an arrow travels from the bow, the more accurate it will be, providing that the arrow is tuned or matched to the bow and flight is stable.

Prior to Hickman's experiments, no one had attempted to collect data regarding changes in bow or arrow design based upon scientific principles. The entire notion and procedure for testing the speed of an arrow as it leaves the bow, in order to affect bow/arrow design, can be credited to Hickman. A 1949 Popular Mechanics article about Hickman observed:

> The scientific sages ignored the improvements of man's earliest weapon until 1929.
>
> In that year, Dr. C.N. Hickman published the first scientific paper on archery--"Velocity and Acceleration of Arrows." During the last two decades, a span infinitesimal in the vast history of archery--more has been done to improve the bow and arrow than in the entire 50,000 year existence of the weapon.[9]

In order to utilize the spark chronograph most effectively and ac-curately, Hickman realized that the results must be reproducible at will. Therefore, he designed a mechanical shooting device into which a bow

could be mounted, eliminating the human error associated with drawing
and releasing the bow. As far as can be determined, the Shooting
Machine was built in 1927, and was the first of its type.

The Shooting Machine he designed was constructed to duplicate
human movement as much as possible. The bow was clamped onto an
arm that pivoted, and the device which held the string was locked into

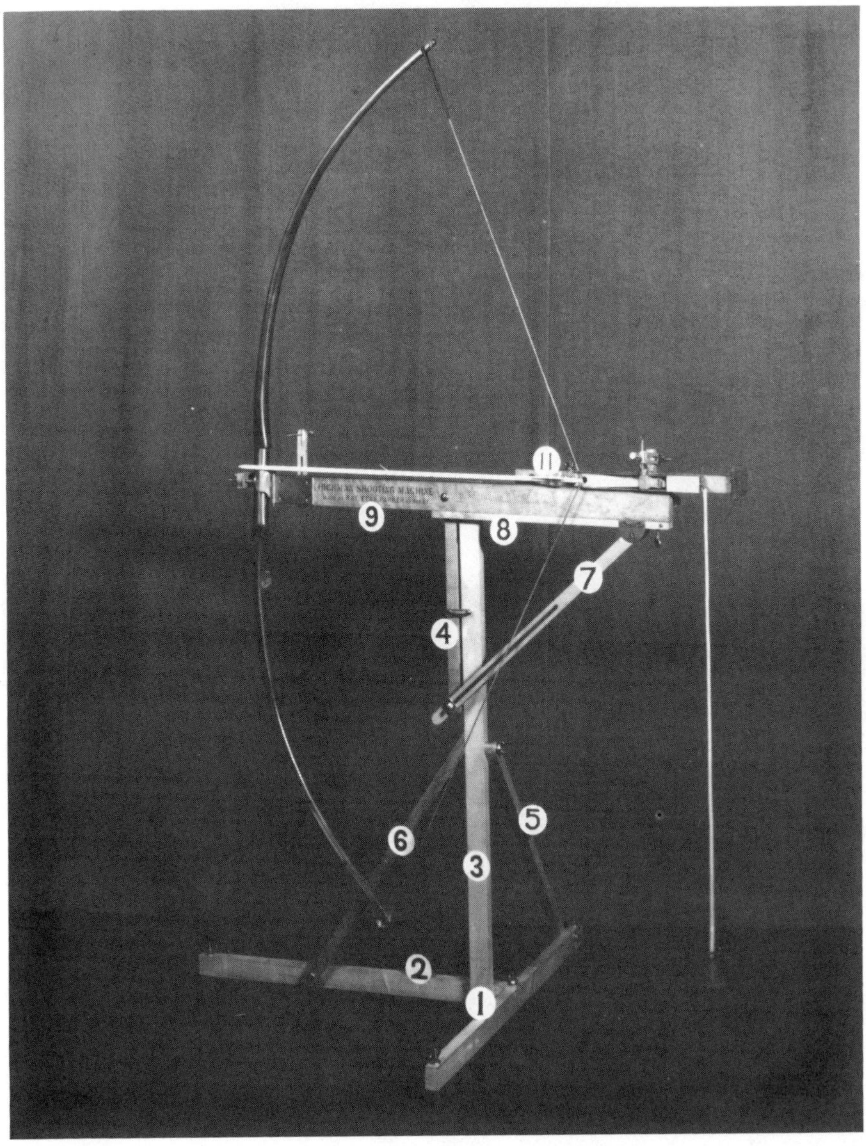

Fig. 38 Hickman Shooting Machine

63

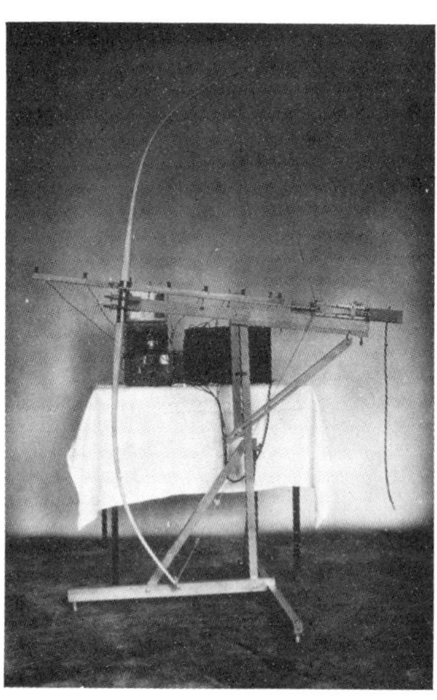

Fig. 39 Shooting Machine and Spark Chronograph

Fig. 40 Hickman Checking Arrow Velocity by Shooting Through Foil Screens.

position with a trigger. In order to assure the smoothest release possible, the trigger was released pneumatically by squeezing a bulb, similar to a camera action. Using good arrows, the device was able to shoot "golds" (center of target) consistently at 50 to 60 yards. The machine folded and fit neatly into a box and was easily carried. It came with two sets of feet, rubber for indoors, and wire that could be bolted into the ground for outdoor use. It was equipped with a front and rear sight, similar to a rifle, for most accurate trajectory settings. The felt pad at the back of the machine was for pulling against the body when cocking the machine (bracing the bow). This device, used in conjunction with the Spark Chronograph, enabled Hickman to make most of his early scientific studies. For most of his tests, the Shooting Machine was equipped with sets of electrical contacts, which were closed by a silver pin on the arrow as it left the bow. The contacts were placed in such a manner and quantity that a space-time curve could be plotted from the chronograph readings. In addition to the space-time curves, Hickman also checked the velocity of the arrow by shooting the arrow through tin foil screens that were two feet apart. The accompanying photographs show the Shooting Machine, the Machine attached to Spark Chronograph, and the Machine set to release an arrow through the foil screens.[10]

By utilizing the combination of Spark Chronograph and Shooting Machine, Hickman was able to perform a variety of tests affecting bow and arrow performance. In 1929, he first published an article, "Velocity and Acceleration of Arrows."[11] It was quickly followed by many others, including, "Effect of Bracing Height of Bows on Static Strains and Stresses," "Effect of String Weight on Arrow Velocity and Efficiency of Bows," " Effect of Bow Length on Static Strains and Stresses," and "Effect of Weight and Air Resistance of Bow Tips on Cast of a Bow."[12]

After completing batteries of tests with the chronograph and shooting machine, it soon became evident to Hickman that the design of bows he was testing could be improved:

> Judging by the general shape of the acceleration curve for all of the various bows which have been tested in the laboratory, it is believed that there is an opportunity of further increasing the efficiency of a bow by changing its design. The acceleration curves are too steep at the beginning and do not hold up well enough toward the end. It is believed that this condition can be improved.[13]

One of the most significant studies having a great impact on the sport of archery was the work done in preparation for his article, "Fiber Stresses in Bows."[14] In this he showed that the very popular English long bow was one of the least efficient designs for energy storage and durability. He proved that the semi-circular cross-section of the long bow caused great stress on the bow limbs, causing a short life span.

Hickman had often said that a physicist could look at the design of the long bow and immediately point out faults in its construction. He maintained that the design was based upon art, rather than science. His experiments with arrow velocity and fiber stresses caused him to seek new bow designs. He was looking for a bow that would give the cast (speed and distance) of an 80-90 pound bow for flight shooting but would have a pull of much lower weight. Hickman had become interested in flight shooting, or shooting for distance, but could not pull the 90 pounds or more necessary to participate successfully.

When he was younger, Hickman had made and shot with flat bows, as opposed to the English long bow with the rounded belly. Flat bows (see Fig. 41) had been made by the Indians and by most civilizations, but at the time Hickman was experimenting, the English long bow was the style of bow most often produced in the United States.[15] He designed experiments to test the flat bow, and shared his findings in several articles written in 1932, including "Effect of Thickness and Width of a Bow on Its Form of Bending," and "The Neutral Plane of Bending of a Bow."[16] At the time, the articles on arrow velocity and fiber stresses were not well received by bow makers, who continued to produce the English long bow. However, as archers who read the articles attempted to make and shoot with flat bows, one by one the tackle makers converted to the flat-bellied bow.[17]

After years of testing, Hickman applied for a patent on a bow with very different design features. The 1935 patent showed that the new design of the bow increased the power of the bow to cast or send an arrow. The chief benefit of this feature was that a person could pull a lighter bow and get the advantage of pulling a heavier one. Thus, the arrow would travel to the target faster and be less influenced by wind or human error. The bow had highly reflexed, recurved limbs, curving away from the archer when not at full draw, and resembling the number 3. When at full draw, the limbs straightened out and the string made an angle of 90 degrees with the tips of each limb. This design allowed the use of very long arrows with the short limbs, helping to gain velocity and distance. There was very little stress on the bow limbs. The bracing height, or distance from string to bow handle when bow was strung, varied according to the weight of the arrow, giving more nearly constant acceleration. This was possibly the first attempt to "tune" the arrow to the bow, something that is done as a matter of course today. The bow limbs were composite limbs, which gave them twice the power of single

DIMENSIONS of SOME ACTUAL BOWS

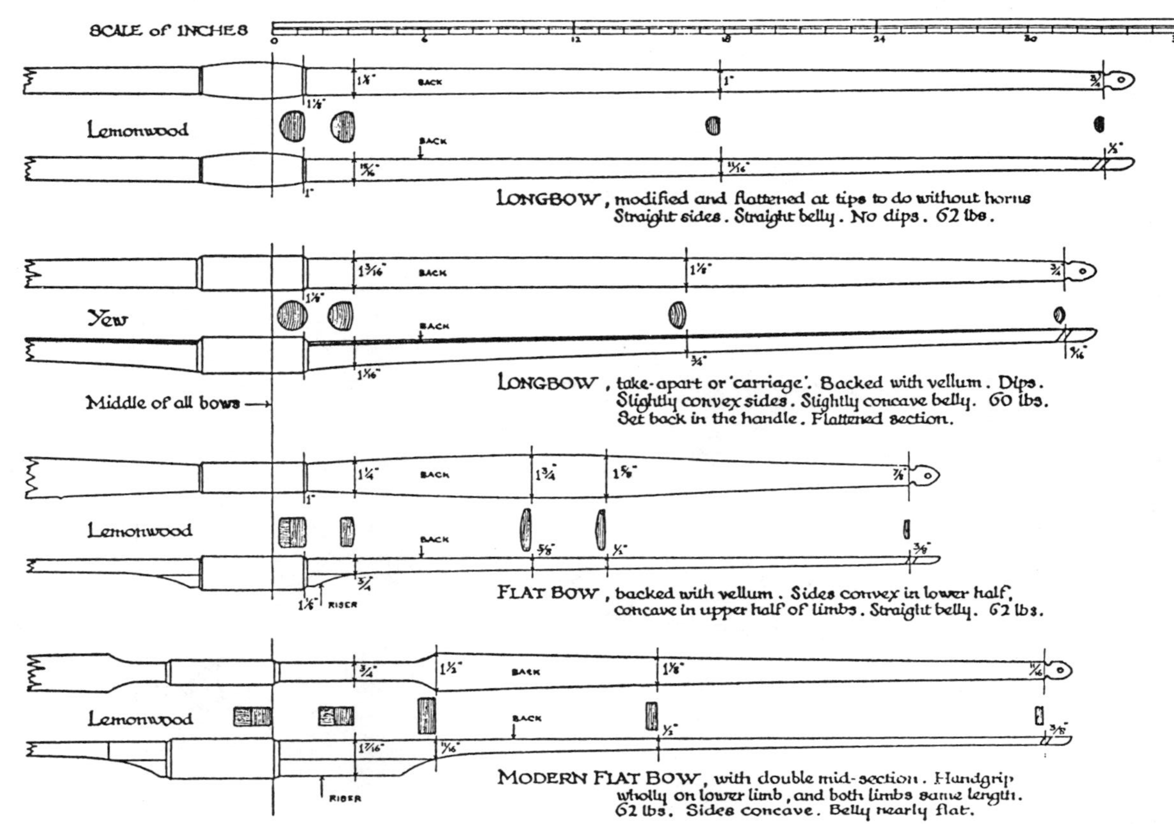

Fig. 41

67

piece limbs. Due to the handle and limb designs, it was very nearly a
center shot bow, so that the arrow travelled as close to the center of the
bow as possible and did not have to snake around the bow.[18] (Fig. 42, 43,
44, 45, 46)

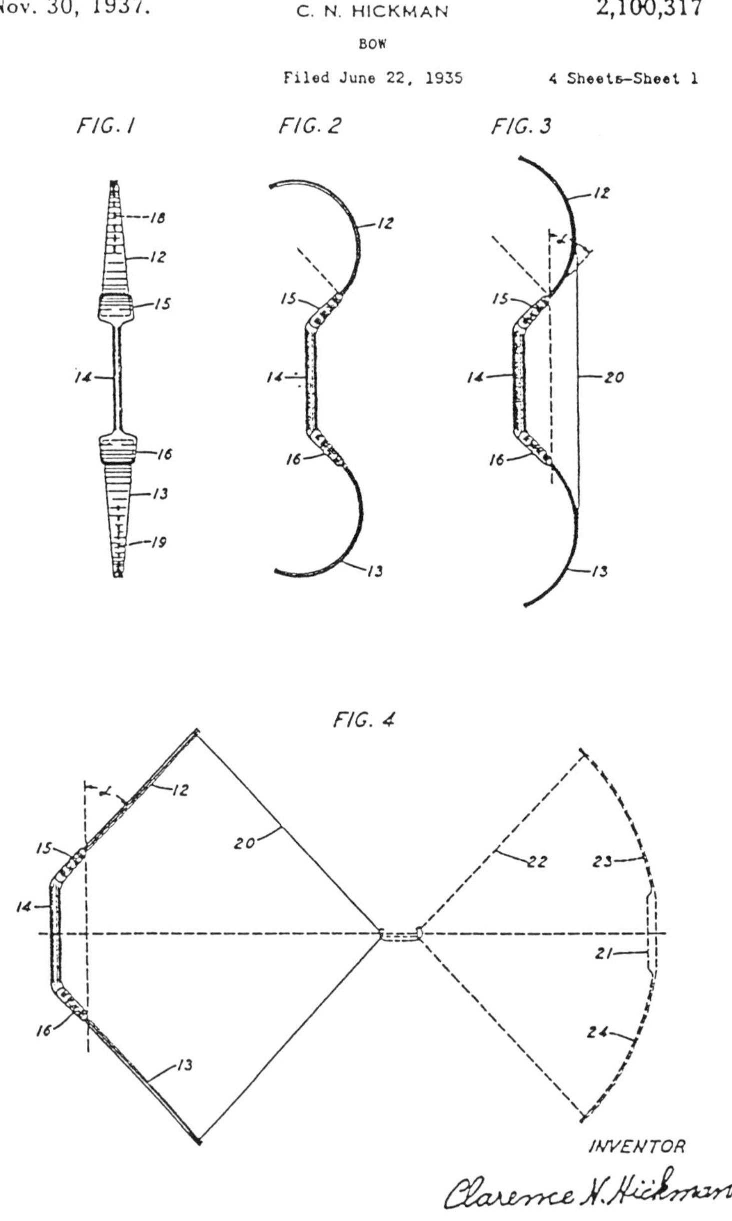

Fig. 42 Schematic of New Bow

Earlier bows made by Hickman were technically all a form of center shot. The Indians used this design, and Hickman's father always cut a piece out of the bow for the arrow. Since Hickman shot with the left eye and used an extended sideways sight, he cut only a small portion for the arrow. Another bowyer, or maker of bows, Bill Folberth, first made a design where a bow sight could be used in the cut-out portion of the bow.[19]

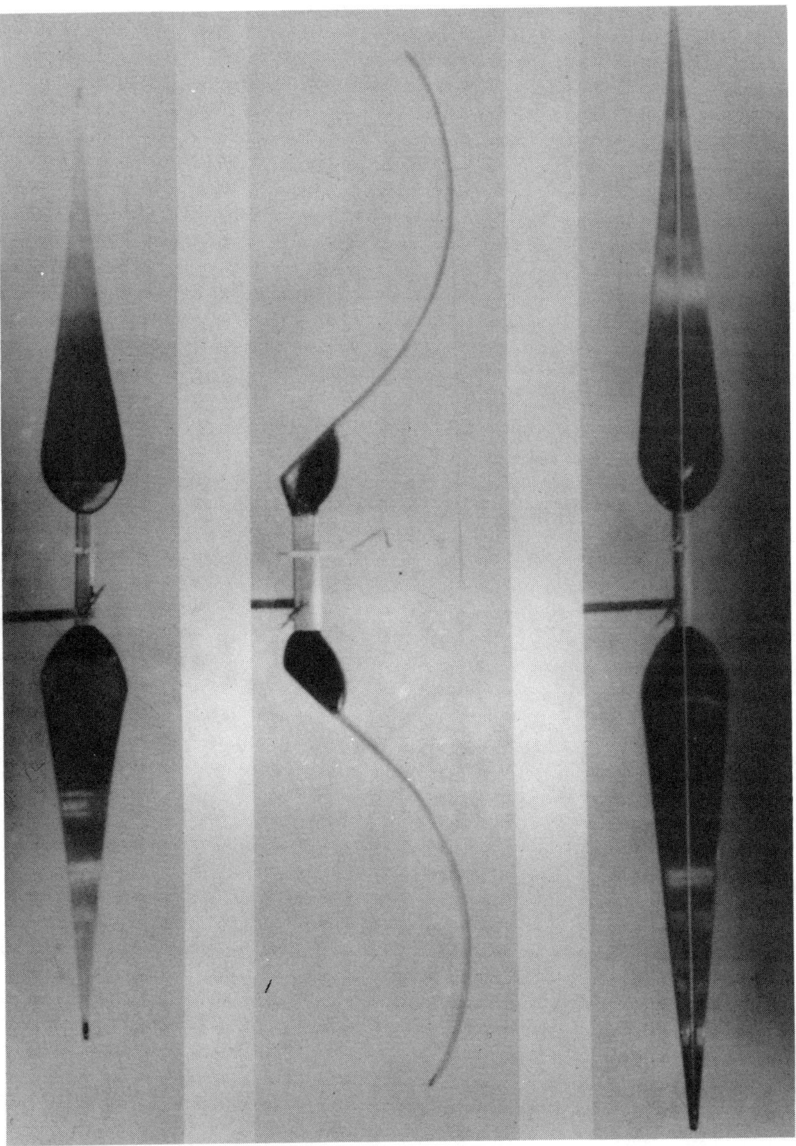

Fig. 43 HICKMAN BOW OF "RADICAL DESIGN"

Fig. 44 Standard Bow of Period (Modified by Hickman)

Fig. 45 Hickman's Bow of "Radical Design"

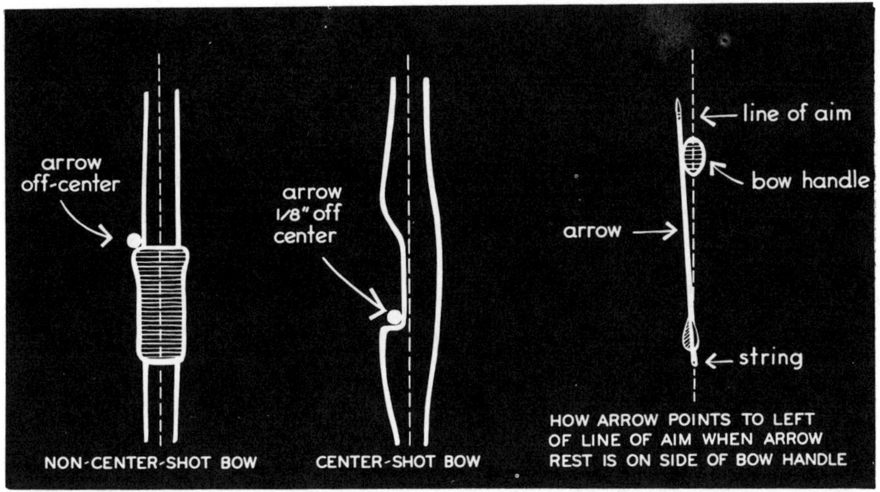

Fig. 46 Comparison of Center-Shot and Non-Center Shot Bow

In order to clearly show the advantages of the new bow, the following figures contrast designs of bows used in the 1930's with earlier styles:

Fig. 47

Most bows in use in 1935 had this shape.
a) The unbraced bow was approximately straight
   (no curvature of limbs).
b) When braced, it was subjected to considerable stress. After being used for some time, these bows took on a permanent set, which decreased the cast of the bow.
c) Bow in fully drawn position.

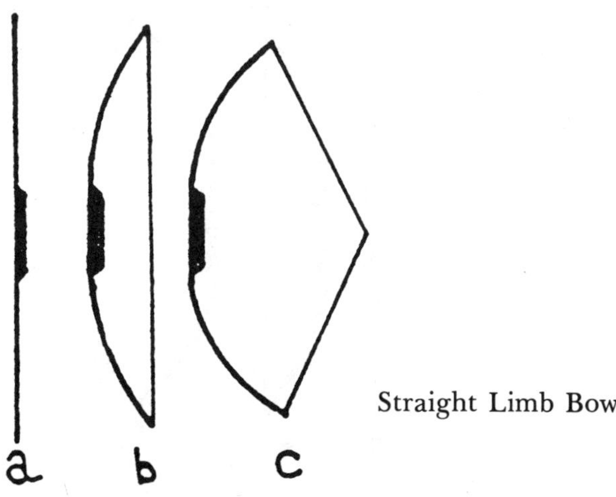

Fig. 48

In order to offset the effect of the permanent set, the limbs
were often given a set in the opposite direction. It looked the same as
the bow in Figure 47, but in the braced position it possessed more
potential energy. For the same holding force, this bow had higher
fiber stresses than the first bow.

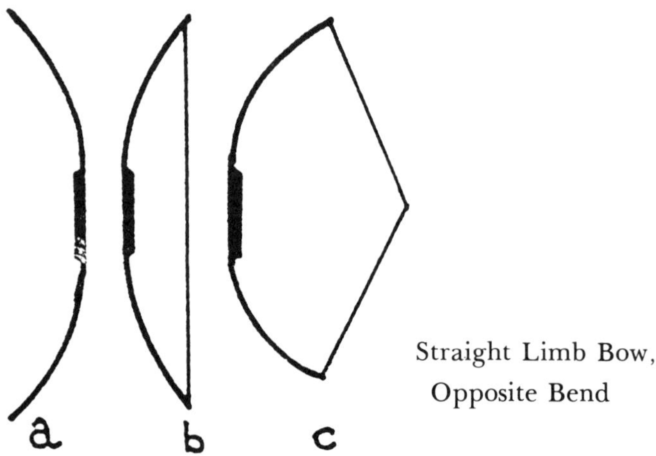

Straight Limb Bow,
Opposite Bend

Fig. 49

Some bows were fitted with tips which were curved back as shown.
Those bows had the same stresses as the bow in Figure 48.

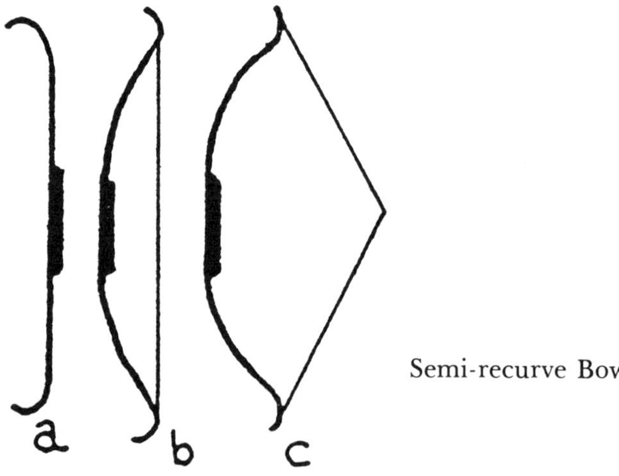

Semi-recurve Bow

Fig. 50

Many Asiatic bows had both of the foregoing features. These bows were highly reflexed and were also fitted with curved tips. The Turkish bow is an example of this type of construction. The work that can be obtained from this bow is much greater than could be obtained from the other styles having the same holding force, on the other hand, the fiber stresses were also much greater.

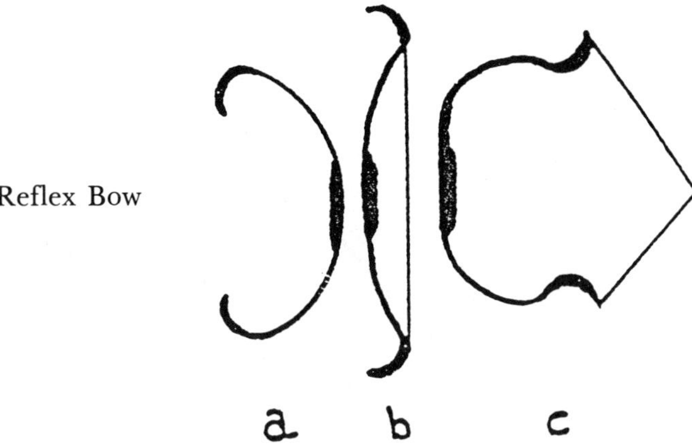

Reflex Bow

Fig. 51

There was one more form of construction that had often been used. In order to construct the highly reflexed limbs, it was necessary to use two or more layers (a composite form of construction). In cases where the limbs were made of a single piece of wood, they could not be highly reflexed so they were often set back at an angle with the handle as shown. Pitching the limbs back at an angle gave the bow more potential energy in its braced position. This bow also had higher fiber stresses.

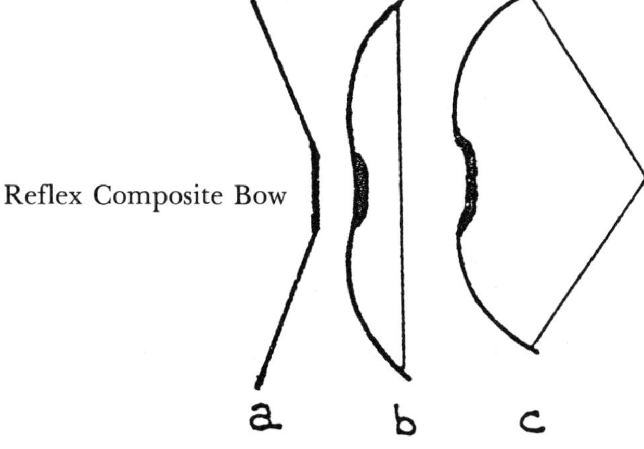

Reflex Composite Bow

This shows Hickman's new bow design, a deflexed, recurve centershot bow. It had composite limbs and could be taken down into two pieces, and had very low fiber stress on the limbs. It had a 100% increased efficiency over the first bow pictured.

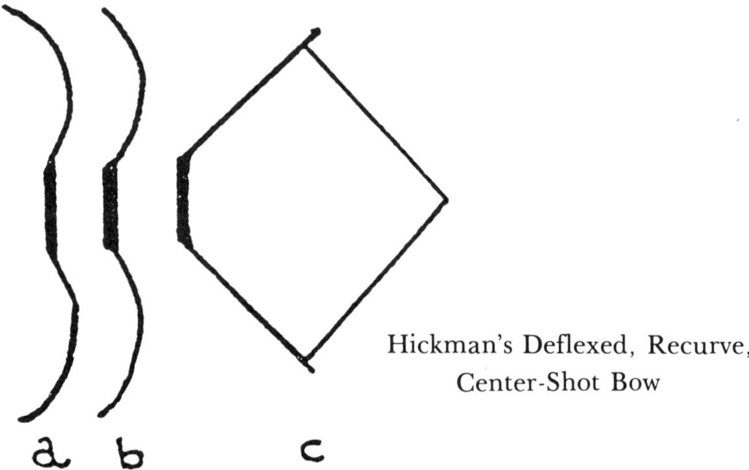

Hickman's Deflexed, Recurve, Center-Shot Bow

Hickman was one of the first modern bowmen to consistently use a two-piece or take-down bow design, and he incorporated it into the new bow also. He wanted to carry his bow in a small case and devised ways to have it come apart. Only since 1970 have most bows on the market incorporated this feature. While designing the take-down bows, Hickman had to carefully devise a way for the bow to fit together, without sacrificing the efficiency of the bow. He was also concerned about the shape of the handle and the pressure of the hand on the bow. Since he was missing fingers on the bow hand, his own grip pressure was not constant. His handle design, he said, allowed him to compensate for this:

> I used round metal handles. I devised an attached handle that surrounded the original handle. A brass tube served the purpose of a handle or grip. This tube was pivoted to a sleeve which in turn could be set up in any position on the original handle and be held by a set screw. With this attachment the pressure could be applied on either side of the center line of the bow and changed at will to fit a change in the bow or method of release. The movable handle could also be raised or lowered to compensate for slight variations

in the manner in which the two limbs attached. Using this attachment it made no difference how you gripped the handle, the pressure was always applied to the bow in exactly the same manner.[21]

Hickman intended his newly designed bow to be used only for flight shooting. In 1946, he entered the New Jersey Flight Shooting Championship in the 50 lb. class. He used his new 25 lb. bow, and came in second, shooting farther than all others in the 50 lbs. class.[22] Many people, impressed with the bow's efficiency after reading his articles or watching him shoot, tried to use it for target shooting. At the time, it was not stable enough to be used exactly as designed for target purposes; however, the principles incorporated in Hickman's new bow would eventually be used by every American manufacturer of bows. Dr. Paul E. Klopsteg, noted scientist and archer, was one of the first persons to recognize the importance of and agree with Hickman's bow design concepts. First to modify the bow for target shooting were Bill Folberth of Cleveland, Ohio and Bill Jackson of Robin Hood Archery Company, Montclair, New Jersey.[23]

Perhaps Hickman's greatest contribution to the sport of archery was demonstrating the importance of scientific inquiry and procedures in the development of more efficient equipment. His publications and ability to physically demonstrate his findings caused bowyers and archers to become more aware of and interested in the variety of his archery discoveries and inventions.

REFERENCES

1. Clarence N. Hickman, "Archery Activities of C.N. Hickman," August 1954, Hickman Archives; and taped Interview with Clarence N. Hickman, Jackson Heights, N.Y., September 10, 1979, in the writer's possession.
2. Hickman, "Archery Activities of C.N. Hickman."
3. Clarence N. Hickman, Letter to Paul Klopsteg, Glenview, Illinois, April 15, 1962, p.3, Hickman Archives.
4. Clarence N. Hickman, Letter to John P. Craven, Chief Scientist, Department of the Navy, July 18, 1961, Hickman Archives.
5. *Webster's New Collegiate Dictionary*, (Springfield, Mass.: G & C Merriam Co. 1979), p.197.
6. Clarence N. Hickman, "A Portable Spark Chronograph for Use on Either Direct of Alternating Current," *Journal of the Franklin Institute*, 211 (January 1931):64.
7. Clarence N. Hickman, Paul Klopsteg, and Forrest Nagler, *Archery, The Technical Side*, (Milwaukee: North American Press, 1947), p.12.
8. Earl Hoyt Jr., President, Hoyt Archery Company, Missouri, Letter to Clarence Hickman, January 29, 1959, p.2, Hickman Archives.
9. Morris Chaklai and Allan Rechtschaffen, "Science Hits the Bull's Eye," *Popular Mechananics Magazine*, 91 (March 1949): 174.
10. Clarence N. Hickman, "Velocity and Acceleration of Arrows, Weight and Efficiency of Bows as Affected by Backing of Bow." *Journal of the Franklin Institute*, 208(October 1929):522-23.
11. *Ibid.*
12. Clarence N. Hickman, "Effect of Bracing Height of Bows on Static Strains and Stresses," *Ye Sylvan Archer*, (March 1931):7-11;
Clarence N. Hickman, "Effect of String Weight on Arrow Velocity and Efficiency of Bows," *Ye Sylvan Archer*, (April 1931):6-9;
Clarence N. Hickman, "Effect of Bow Length on Static Strains and Stresses," Ye Sylvan Archer, (August 1931):3-4, 10-11; and
Clarence N. Hickman, "Effect of Weight and Air Resistance of Bow Tips on Cast of a Bow," Ye Sylvan Archer, (September 1931): 3-4-7, Hickman Archives.
13. Clarence N. Hickman, "Velocity and Acceleration of Arrows...," p. 537.
14. Clarence N. Hickman, "Fiber Stresses in Bows," *Ye Sylvan Archer*, (March 1932):7-10, Hickman Archives.
15. Hodgkin, Adrian, The Archer's Craft, (N.Y.: A.S. Barnes and Company, 1968), p.76.
16. Clarence N. Hickman, "Effect of Thickness and Width of a Bow on Its Form of Bending," *Ye Sylvan Archer* (January 1932):5-8,14; and Clarence N. Hickman, "The Neutral Plane of Bending of a Bow," *Ye Sylvan Archer*, (February 1932):3-5, Hickman Archives.

17. Clarence N. Hickman, Letter to Earl Hoyt, Jr., "Comments on Significant Advancements in Modern Bow Design," July 31, 1961, 3 pages. Hickman Archives.

18. Hochman, Louis, *The Complete Archery Book*, (N.Y.: Arco Publishing Co., 1965), p.8.

19. Clarence N. Hickman, letter to Earl Hoyt, Jr. "Comments on Significant Advancements...," Hickman Archives.

20. Clarence N. Hickman, Paul Klopsteg, Forrest Nagler, *Archery, The Technical Side*, pp. 50,51,62.

21. Clarence N. Hickman, "Critical Bows," July 1955 (Unpublished), Hickman Archives.

22. Chaklai and Rechtschaffen, pp. 176-177.

23. Clarence N. Hickman, Letter to Early Hoyt, Jr., "Comments on Significant Advancements...," Hickman Archives.

CHAPTER

IV

HICKMAN: ARCHERY INNOVATOR

The Spark Chronograph and Shooting Machine, and the experiments which were conducted using them, ultimately resulted in the New Bow Design; however, those first experiments and the countless others that followed were to result in many more archery contributions. Hickman continued to "give" to the archery field for approximately forty years, earning the title of "Father of Scientific Archery."[1] The following are selected examples of the diverse ways in which he was able to refine the art and science of archery for both archers and manufacturers of archery equipment.

In his first published archery experiment, "Velocity and Acceleration of Arrows,"[2] Hickman investigated the effect of bow backing on the velocity and acceleration of arrows as well as on the weight and efficiency of the bow. For centuries it had been the custom of bowmakers, even those in primitive tribes, to place some sort of substance on the back of the bow to decrease the probability of breaking it. A variety of substances had been used, such as raw hide, sinew, and hickory and other wood strips. While Hickman was concerned about the bow fracturing, he was also interested in determining if the efficiency of the bow could be enhanced by selected backings. The increase in efficiency would enable the archer to shoot the arrow farther and faster without proportionately increasing the force required to draw the string. Hickman decided to test various types of backing by weighing the bows (determining the force required to draw them), and then shooting arrows of different weights with them, using his mechanical Shooting Machine to hold the bows. The velocities of the arrows were determined, and the efficiency of the bow was calculated. He used various types of bows (lemonwood, yew, hickory, osage orange) and various backings (rawhide, fiber, bakelite). Although he was able to prove that reinforcing the bow would increase the efficiency, it was some time before he hit on the most efficient material.

79

Although rawhide had been used as a bow backing in ancient times, his experiments showed that unless it was applied just right, it actually increased the strength required to draw the string, without greatly increasing the distance or the speed with which the arrow travelled. Hickman kept searching for backing materials, and in the early 1930's found, through testing, that untwisted silk was an effective backing material. It was high in tensile strength, easy to apply, reasonable in price, and attractive in appearance. Silk had not been used for backing in the past because it was difficult to apply. As a woven cloth, it was worthless for backings.

Not until Hickman invented and patented a process of manufacturing the silk in sheet form could it be applied with ease and have an attractive appearance. Not only did the silk protect the bow from breaking, but it improved the cast by preventing the bow from "taking a set," that is, staying in the braced position after it had been unbraced. This added greatly to the life of the bow.[3] Hickman found a company that could throw some silk without a twist in the threads. He then designed a machine with drums to make the backing. Essentially, the silk was thrown in threads, without twist, and wound on large spools. The threads were run through a glue bath and laid on two foot diameter drums by a guide travelling back and forth across the drum. Two and three layers of the silk were placed on each other. After the glue had dried, the sheet of silk (12" wide by 6' long) was peeled off the drum.[4] Hickman also discovered that it helped to pre-stretch the silk before applying it, so he designed stretching jigs to accomplish this. Hickman sold the sheets he produced to tackle makers all over the United States. They, in turn, advertised in archery magazines. One such advertisement stated:[5]

HICKMAN'S SILK BACKING STRIPS FOR BOWS

We are the exclusive retail sales agents for the silk backing designed and produced by Dr. C. N. Hickman.

A strip 1¼" wide and 72" long at $1.30 plus 10c for packing and postage. For wider bows, a strip 1¾" wide and 72" long $1.80, plus 10c for packing and postage. Please send cash with order.

We stock 50 percent heavier silk backing which we recommend for all bows over 45lb. Prices are 50 percent more than those listed for the standard weight.

RUSS HOOGERHYDE, Inc.

1865 Shermer Ave., Northbrook, Ill.

Fig. 53
1941 Silk Backing Ad

From 1939 until the supply of silk was cut off after Pearl Harbor, he manufactured 1700 silk sheets, enough to back 11,900 bows. He had eight drums in his apartment, and could make eight sheets in an evening.[6] Originally, Hickman gave the backing away free to his friends, but that started to become a financial burden, due to the increasing demand. A friend who was connected with a tackle maker wanted him to manufacture the backing for the tackle maker. Hickman did not have time to handle such a business; however, Hickman's wife agreed to handle the shipping and billing, and Hickman took care of the technical manufacture. The business was listed in his wife's name, and she kept the small income from the venture. They charged enough to cover materials and handling plus make a small profit. No attempt was made to try to cover exact labor costs.[7] Hickman once stated: "Many a time I wished I had never done this research. I would come home from a hard day at the Lab and find an order for 10 more sheets. I could only make 8 in an evening."[8] Hickman's sense of dedication prevailed, however, and he continued to manufacture the backing until he had no more silk available.

During the war, silk was unavailable because the entire United States supply was being used to manufacture parachutes. Since addi-

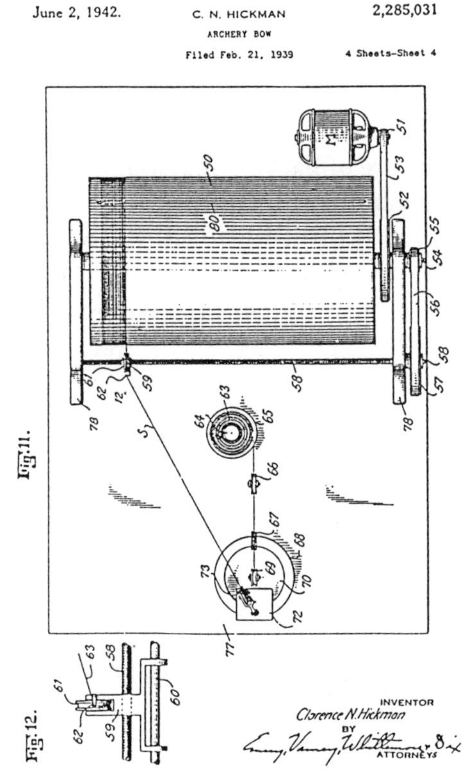

Fig. 54

Machine for producing sheets of silk backing

tional silk was unavailable from Japan, the chief supplier, a new fiber was fabricated for use in the manufacture of parachutes. The Celanese Corporation of Maryland had developed a fiber, Fortisan, which was two or three times as strong as silk. Due to the confidential nature of the material, it was not available for public use until after the war was over; however, because Hickman had a security clearance, he was able to obtain samples of the material and he performed many tests on it. Additionally, at the end of the war he had Forrest Nagler, Chief Mechanical Engineer at Allis-Chalmers Manufacturing Co. in Wisconsin, further test the Fortisan for him. Nagler's results agreed with Hickman's.[9] Hickman realized that the material was much better than silk and prepared an article for release in *American Bowman-Review*, in March 1946.[10] In this article he informed the archery public that silk would cost $24 per pound when thrown in the proper strands for making backing, and it was not yet available. He discussed the properties of Fortisan and recommended its use as a replacement backing for silk. He also bowed to the demand for bow backing by going back into business, and in the same issue ran an ad for the Fortisan. Robin Hood Archery Company, one of the largest dealers, also ran an ad, as they had agreed to sell and apply the new backing. (Fig. 55)

Hickman continued to produce the Fortisan backing until the Korean War when the U.S. Government took all the Fortisan that was being manufactured. During this interval he made 4,531 sheets, enough to back 30,457 bows. After the Korean War, Hickman refused to resume the manufacture of backing material for several reasons. First, it was just too time consuming. Second, at this time fiberglass was available in many forms, and Hickman felt that it would ultimately replace the Fortisan.[12] In 1948, he had done a study of the breaking strength of many fibers, but the properties of the glass were not yet available to him:

The following table gives the breaking strength of several materials when made up into a size corresponding to the Violin D string (No. 3 surgical Catgut)[13]

Materials	Pounds
Wool Fibers	6
Cellulose Acetate (rayon)	8
Horse Hair	15
Cotton Fibers	18
No. 3 Surgical Catgut	20
Silk Fibers	22
Irish Linen	28
Chinese Grass Fibers	32
Nylon	35
Fortisan	42
Glass Fibers	?

FORTISAN
For Backing Bows

FORTISAN is a fiber developed by the Celanese Corporation. The entire output of this product was used for making shrouds for parachutes. It is now available for other purposes. The fiber is about one third the size of silk. It is over twice as strong as silk and has a higher modulus. The fibers are thrown without twist into a strand and manufactured into sheets for backing bows. The sheets are about 11½ inches wide and 72 inches long. There are over 100,000 fibers per inch of width of the backing.

Sheets are now available in thicknesses of .025 and .037 inches. All dealers and tackle makers are permitted to split the sheets and sell to individuals.

C. N. HICKMAN

3536 79th St. Jackson Heights, New York

FORTISAN
BOW BACKINGS

DR. C. N. HICKMAN'S LATEST CONTRIBUTION TO ARCHERY

REJUVENATE YOUR PET BOW — REFLEX THE LIMBS
PROTECT THE BACK — SIMPLE TO APPLY

WILL ADD UP to 15lbs. TO THE DRAWING WEIGHT WITHOUT ADDING ANY NOTICEABLE BULK—FINISHES BEAUTIFULLY

STANDARD STRIPS—72″ long—any width at $1.00 per inch x 72″
HEAVY STRIPS—72″ long—any width at $1.50 per inch x 72″

WE WILL BE GLAD TO BACK YOUR BOW—Write For Prices

SEND FOR 1946 CATALOG

ROBIN HOOD ARCHERY CO.
955 BROAD ST. NEWARK 2, N. J.

Fig. 55 Fortisan Bow Backing Advertisements

Ultimately, as Hickman had predicted, fiberglass would replace Fortisan as the best backing for bows. In the meantime, archers around the country were indebted to Hickman for the years of testing and research which enabled him to provide them with the best bow materials.

When Hickman first worked with the testing of backing, in order to document his results it was imperative that he determine the precise weight of each bow tested. Once again, he developed his own tool, since no accurate measuring device existed. In 1938, Hickman developed a Bow Weighing Machine to perform the necessary tests. Although he had experimented with other types of weighing machines earlier, until that date he had not been able to construct one that completely satisfied him. Since he greatly needed to measure his new bow accurately, he spent much time constructing the weighing device. The accompanying photos show the machine, with a bow being weighed by Dr. Hickman, and a closeup of the machine and graph. (Fig. 56, 57, 58) Although this particular device is not especially essential to the average archer, it was completely necessary for early testing materials. The device itself was mechanically simple but ingenious. As the bow was pulled up into full draw position, the graph panel (#3) slid to the right on two iron rods (#2). The panel slid along the rods at the same rate as the bow was pulled. A curve was therefore traced as the bow was pulled into the full draw and also let down. It thus provided the force draw curve as well as the bow's loss in weight. The differences in the curves enabled Hickman to see which bow designs lost performance due to faulty materials or design and to compare more efficient bows. The machine's design enabled it to work with a single graph paper, sufficient for recording the weights of 40 or more bows, with ample room to label the tracings with pertinent information.[14]

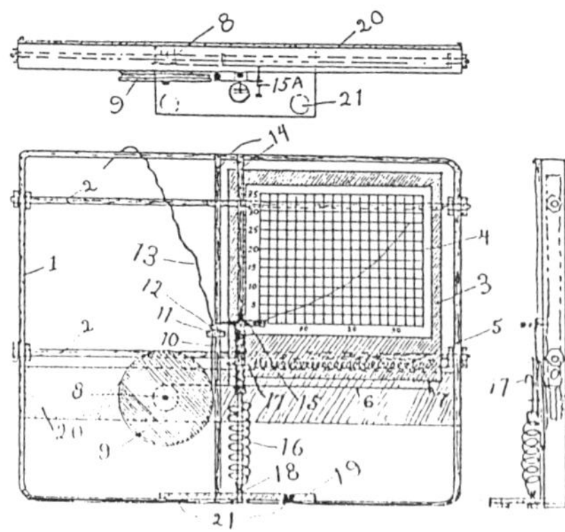

Fig. 56   Schematic of bow weighing machine

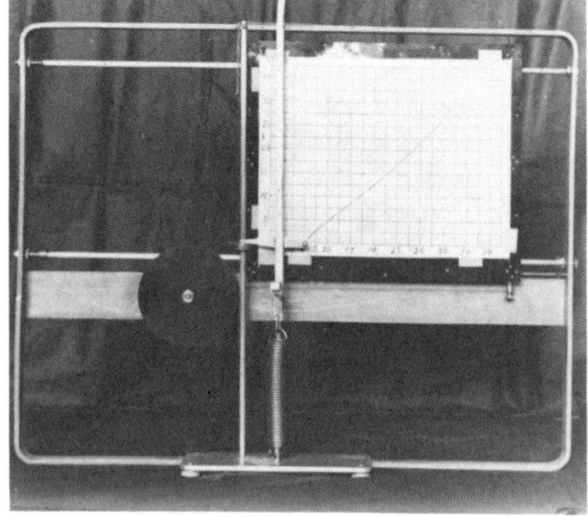

Fig. 57

Hickman's Bow Weighing Machine

Fig. 58

Hickman's Bow Weighing Machine

As important as his backing innovations were to archery, it is probably safe to say that the average archer in the 1950's knew Dr. Hickman's name in connection with the "Archer's Paradox" more than any other of his discoveries. Because of the spectacular visual nature of the results, it is difficult to forget the phenomenon after having seen it.

Archers throughout the world had always speculated about what happens to an arrow as it was leaving the bow. A phenomenon known as The Archer's Paradox had puzzled archers for centuries. When glancing at the bow and arrow, it would seem that the arrow should fly far to the left, since it passes on the left side of the bow, while the string flies down the middle to the point from which it started. Archers knew that the spine, or stiffness and resilience of an arrow, must be matched to the drawing force of a bow if the arrow was to fly correctly, but no one ever knew precisely why. Hickman, continuing to probe the scientific problems of archery, predicted that the phenomenon was due to the manner in which the arrow bent and vibrated as it left the bow.[15] In order to prove this and to study it further, he decided to try to take pictures of an arrow in flight, using the best slow motion methods of the time. The first high-speed archery pictures were taken for Hickman in 1930 by photographer Harry Day on the roof of the Fiske Building in New York, using a 16mm camera with

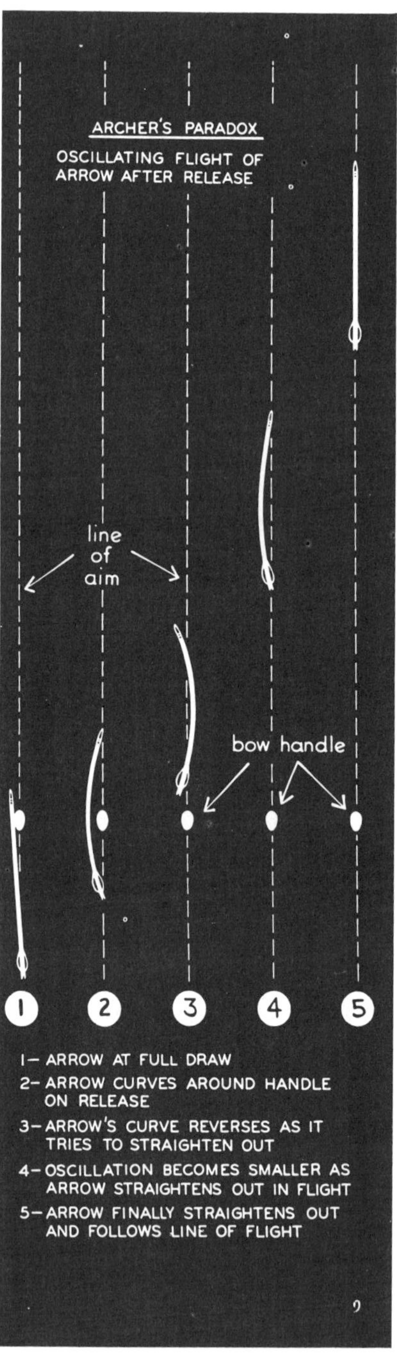

Fig. 59
Archer's Paradox

the speed at 2000 frames per second. Even though the lighting was poor and the distortion due to the optical system was great, the information obtained from the pictures was invaluable.[16] For the first time Hickman had some visual proof to back up his suspicions, and the ideas gained from these photos influenced the design for his new bow. Several years later, about 1938, he obtained permission from the Bell Laboratories to use a 4000 frame-per-second 16mm camera (which he helped design) to photograph the behavior of different types of arrows when shot by expert archers. The pictures shot at 4000 frames-per-second were excellent and nothing like them had ever been seen. Hickman had them reproduced and sent around the country to archery clubs. The pictures were extreme-ly important for two reasons. First, the films showed that the arrow ac-tually bends around the bow and keeps oscillating in its flight toward the target, until it eventually straightens out before hitting the target. This not only solved the academic problem of the Paradox, but also showed why arrows of certain spines (flexibility) must be matched to different weight bows for accurate flight. A badly matched arrow could assume a permanent warp or could break due to the initial buckling from the force of the string.[17]

Fig. 60

Photographs of Arrow Leaving Bow 2000 Frames per Second

Sequence Photos from Archer's Paradox Film (1930)

1. Initial Position during Hold   2. Buckle to left as viewed
by observer in front.

3. Return to straight position from photo 2.

4. Buckle to right as arrow makes 1st half vibration

5. Return to straight position from photo 4

6. Return to left as arrow completes first vibration

7. Return to straight
from photo 6

8. Buckle to right on second
vibration of bow

9. Return to straight
from photo 8

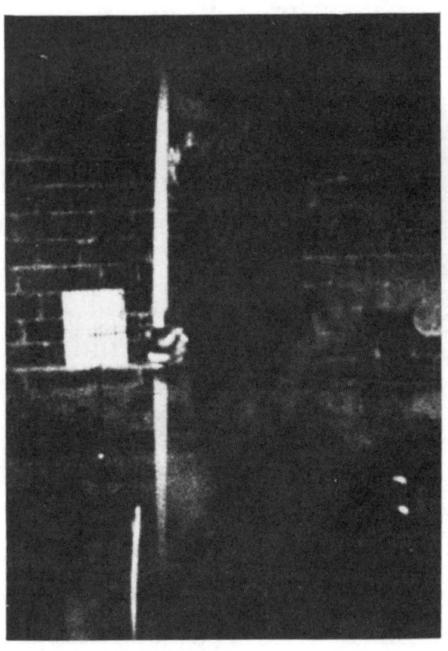

10. Buckle to left as arrow
completes its 2nd vibration

After studying the films, Hickman advocated shooting the arrow from a point nearer the center of the bow rather than from the side of the bow. This "center shot" bow eliminated the need for special considerations in matching arrows of correct spine. The center shot bow had the advantage of allowing a wider range of arrows to be shot from a given bow, because the arrows did not have to bend quite so much around the bow.[19] Hickman utilized this center shot concept in all his bows from the middle thirties on. Only after his second series of films did others start to realize and appreciate the principle. In the 1980's, every bow made is a "center shot" bow to some degree or another, and archers are provided with scientific charts to more accurately match their arrows to specific bows.

Hickman was besieged by requests for more films and realized that besides the expense, he could not continue to monopolize the Bell facilities and equipment. At this point he decided to build his own high-speed camera, capable of running from 200 to 6000 frames per second and operating with 8mm film, which was far less expensive than 16mm. In 1940, he built such a camera. Since he wanted it to be used on the field as well as indoors, the camera was equipped with a Variac for changing the voltage. A series wound motor was used so that the torque became low at low voltages.

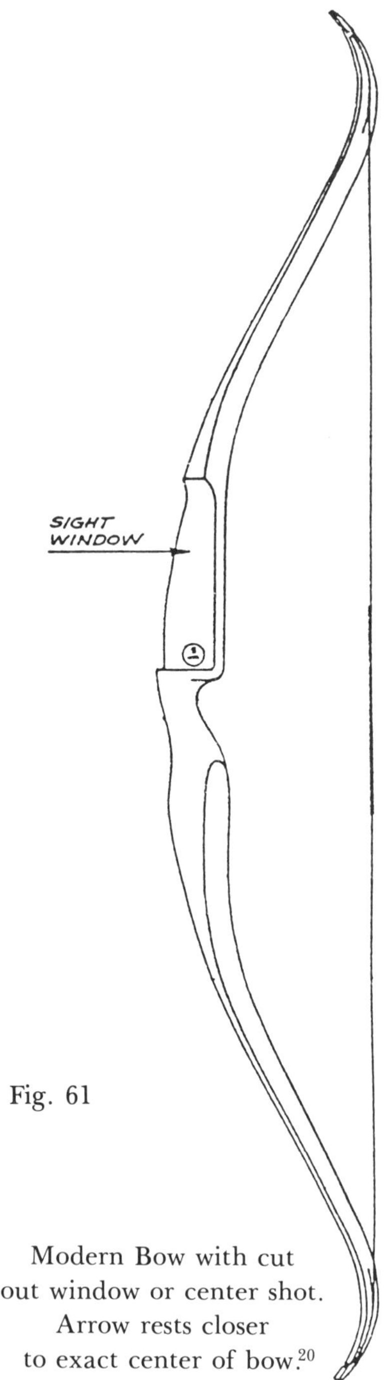

Fig. 61

Modern Bow with cut out window or center shot. Arrow rests closer to exact center of bow.[20]

Fig. 62

Hickman's 8 mm High Speed Camera 1942

The frame speed could not be reduced past 200 frames and still be reliable, but it could be increased to 6000 frames per second at 130 volts.[21] (Fig. 62,63,64)

Just before the United States entered World War II, Hickman finished building the camera. In March 1941, the camera was taken to Washington, D.C. for use in connection with Hickman's rocket research. It was in continuous use photographing rockets until the war ended. It gave such excellent results that Section E of the National Defense Research Committee had five more of the cameras made. Since the camera could be operated by remote control, it was often used to photograph explosions, sometimes only 100 yards away. When electricity wasn't available, a hand crank was designed that allowed the camera to operate at 2000 frames per second. This camera was replaced, for various special tests, by the Ribbon Frame Camera later developed by Hickman. It wasn't until 1947 that Hickman was able to use that precise camera for more archery films. Its low cost, speed, flexibility, and portability made it an extremely attractive camera for use with future archery experiments.[22]

Fig. 63

8mm High Speed Camera --
Front View

Fig. 64

8mm High Speed
Camera Threading
Mechanism and
Daylight Loading
Spool

Dr. Robert P. Elmer, who in 1946 wrote the authoritative best seller *Target Archery,* wrote to Hickman with a request:

> I have done all the main work (for the book) except the Archer's Paradox; my time limit being June 30th. In as much as your 4000 frames per second movies have put all other work on the subject in the limbo of the past, I am wondering if there is any way in which I can get those films to study....It seems a pity to have a big book like this one put on the market when it contains no more than I can hash up about the Paradox except what I remember about your films and can glean from your articles in the *American Bowman-Review.*[23]

Hickman sent the films, and bows and arrows would never be the same again. Neither would the archers of the time who were privileged to watch an arrow snake out of a bow in slow motion.

Hickman's contributions to strengthening bows and to understanding of the aerodynamics of the arrow may have been his greatest archery innovations, but he was also interested in other aspects of archery, such as the skills involved in shooting the bow. One skill which presented problems was aiming. From his earliest experiments he had been working with better methods of aiming an arrow. For centuries, archers had been using what is often called the "instinctive" method of aiming. This simply meant the archer looked at the object to be hit, aimed at it, and through practice "knew" whether to aim higher or lower for given distances from the target. This required much practice and had little precision.

It is not known exactly when the first sighting aids in archery were used, but it seems as though the first person to write about them was Horace Ford of England, who in 1856 wrote an article entitled "Archery, Its Theory and Practice."[24] In it he described a method which came to be known as the "point-of-aim" method of sighting at the target. With this method he set records that stood for forty years or more. Basically, it involved the archer drawing the string back until his hand was under his chin, and the string stopped at his chin. (This stopping place is called an "anchor.") Since the eye was on a higher level than the arrow, the line of sight was downward from the eye to the arrow point to some point or object on the ground. If the arrow was to be aimed higher, the object was moved farther from the archer. If it was to be aimed lower, the object was moved nearer the archer. By trial and error the object was moved until the arrows hit the center of the target. This method worked much better and was much more consistent than a purely instinctive method of aiming, but it did have some drawbacks. One of these was the fact that new archers did not like to aim at the ground instead of what they wanted to hit. They would have preferred to aim at the target, which they never looked at using this "point-of-aim" method, unless they were at "point blank" range, and could aim directly at the target.[25]

Hickman decided to experiment with a mechanical sight on the bow. Some sights were already in existence, and although they allowed the archer to sight directly at the target, they also had some problems. Basically, the sight on the bow consisted of a bead or pin which could be moved up or down the bow and also adjusted laterally. The early simple sight method had the problem of the archer tilting the top of the bow and having the arrow go right or left, even though the pin was right on the mark. Since the bows did not have the power to project an arrow as today's ,modern bows do, often the sight had to be lowered so much to reach a far distance that the hand blocked the sight. In 1928, Hickman devised a bow sight that was mounted on an extension of the bow rest and placed far enough to the left to enable the left eye to be used. (Fig. 65) For long ranges the bead of the sight was turned down, and for short ranges it was placed above the arrow rest. With this sight it was always possible to sight at the target. At about the same time, prism sights started to come on the market. A simple prism with cross hairs was placed on the bow so that it could be raised or lowered. For long ranges the wider portion of the prism would be down, for shorter ranges, the wedge was placed above the crosshairs. Again, the problem with this sight was that the archer could not see the tip of the arrow, and the length of the draw could not be accurately checked. Some archers, using any of the above sights, tried to correct the problem by placing mirrors on the bows as a "draw check" to see the point of their arrow; however, this further complicated the set-up or working organization of the bow parts and the aiming process.[26]

In the late 1930's, Hickman solved the problem for himself and shared it with others through his articles. He invented a sight consisting of two prisms which bent the light of the target up to the eye. The archer adjusted the prisms until he could aim at the center of the target for the distance at which he was standing. The arrow actually rested on the arm of the sight, and the archer could line up the point of the arrow with the cross hairs of the prism sight and the center of the target; therefore, he had a built in draw check and could not pull the arrow back too little or too far. With this device, any tilting of the bow was immediately observed in the prism sight and eliminated another problem. This sight had all the advantages of the point-of-aim method of aiming, and in addition had the advantage that the archer could look at the object at which he was shooting.[27] (Fig. 66)

Hickman changed his sight one more time, by adding a third prism

Fig. 65

Early Hickman Bow Sight (1928)

to the two prism sight sometime during World War II. (Fig. 67,68) The third prism made it possible to change the sight for windage (horizontal corrections) without making any change in the elevation. This was a vast improvement over the previous method in which any change in one affected the other. The third prism also made it possible to use weaker prisms, or prisms with a lower degree of magnification, so the scale was less critical and the bow could be held steadier. Hickman further improved the three prism sight by providing a means of elevating the whole prism assembly to match the particular bow being used. This allowed the archer to line up the arrow with a black spot in the middle of the center prism, further improving the accuracy of the sight.[28] Hickman shot with the three prism sight, and many archers adopted his technique. At the present time, prism sights are illegal for competition, and they are not quite as necessary due to the improvement in cast and sighting of the modern day bow.

Fig. 66   Hickman 2-prism Bow Sight

By the beginning of World War II, Hickman had concentrated on analyzing the complex technical problems of archery. In the middle forties he began to encounter a problem that was more psychological in nature. This problem, known as "freezing" in the archery world, refers to a condition of stopping before reaching the point of aim necessary to hit the target. This seems to be due to a subconscious fear that the shooter will release the arrow as soon as the tip of the arrow reaches the point of aim, thus deflecting the arrow in the direction the bow is moving.

Hickman attempted to analyze what caused an archer to "freeze," and also suggested some remedies that he had been working on. Briefly

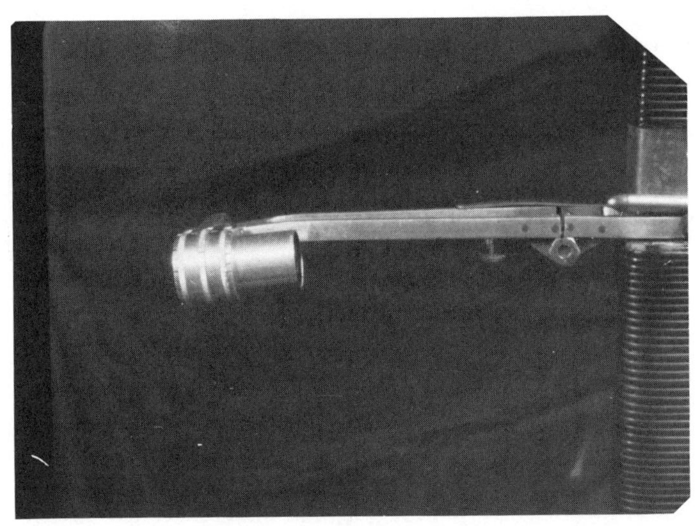

Fig. 67

Hickman 3-prism Bowsight

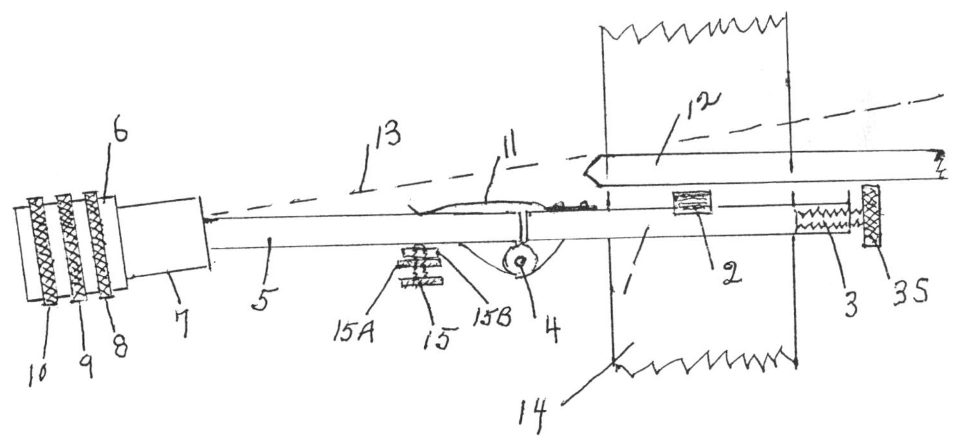

Fig. 68

Sketch of 3-prism sight

summarized, Hickman's analysis of the problem was as follows:

> With minor differences, this is what happens to the archer. In the beginning, he holds on the point or the gold and thinks about all the things that he is supposed to do and then releases when he thinks that he is ready or until, in case he is over-bowed, he can hold no longer. In any case the process of getting ready to shoot takes less and less time so that soon he is popping arrows into the target with the greatest of ease. This goes on for a long time and finally there comes a time when he decides, either through his own good judgment, or the suggestion of a fellow archer, that he is shooting too fast, that he is not holding long enough to get settled down. . . .He decides that he should hold on the gold or point of aim for awhile before releasing. This he attempts to do and is puzzled by the fact that as soon as he is on the point, the release automatically takes place. He just can't hold at all. This stage in which the archer finds himself is what might be called the Inability to Hold. . . .If the archer is determined to learn to hold, the more he tries, the harder it seems to become. To be sure, he can hold if he knows that he is not going to shoot at all, but as soon as he knows that he is going to shoot for a given draw, away it goes as soon as he is on his point. Now comes the next stage in the battle and it is much worse than the first one. Subconscious fear that he will release as soon as he is on the point causes him to pause, below, above, or to one side of the point, according to his own method of getting on the point. This pause gets longer and longer and it seems that the archer has no ability to move the bow arm on to the point. This is what is called freezing. . . .Unless one has experienced this difficulty, it is impossible to imagine the torture one goes through in trying to get on the point, then hold and release at will.[29]

Hickman, who was suffering from the common "freezing" malady, also realized that if someone stood next to him and told him when to release, he could aim at the gold and release when told. In other words, if the responsibility for releasing were removed, the archer could aim. He therefore devised a system that would tell him when to release. The device consisted of an Eastman kodak pneumatic antenna release. The release could be set for times up to 15 seconds. When it released, the clicking noise could readily be heard. At first Hickman wore the device around his neck, but later transferred it to his wrist (See photo.). Hickman would set the timer for a different time each shot, and he never knew precisely when it was going to release. He gave himself approximately 10 seconds, however, so he was sure he had enough time to draw and get ready on the gold. When he first used the camera timer, there were objections because other archers were disturbed by the noise. He found a way to make it so quiet that only he could hear it.[30] (Fig. 69)

Fig. 69   Hickman Timer -- "Freezing" Aid (On Wrist)

While trying to practice holding the bow and not releasing it until he was ready, Hickman developed a further problem. He found that it was necessary to actually make a release when trying to use will power to practice disciplining one's actions; for example, an archer trying to practice in an apartment, who is up at full draw and aimed at a target on the wall, is not really practicing because he knows he cannot release the string. To release a string without an arrow in it would damage the bow, as too much energy would go back into the bow limbs. Thus, in trying to conquer the freezing problem, Hickman designed another archer's aid, the Double String Bow. (Fig. 70) He described the aid in this manner:

> I take a bow that is somewhat heavier than the one I shoot on the range and brace it using a heavy string. I then add another string of sufficient length so that when it is pulled, the limbs are flexed only a short distance. I made the string of sufficient length so that I pull it only about two inches in making the full draw. When this string is pulled in this manner, the other string becomes slack. At will, I release the long string and the other string takes the force required to stop the limbs. This does not damage the bow as it is

99

about the same as pulling the regular string back only a short distance. If you use a sight, you can pull the bow and take sight at any object in the room and make a real release.[31]

Fig. 70 Hickman "Freezing" Aid --
Double String Bow

Of all the 47 articles that Hickman wrote for archery magazines, the article on "Freezing" brought the greatest response. He received hundreds of letters from archers all over the world who could readily identify with the problem, and appreciated some suggested solutions. Besides the fact that Hickman himself had the problem of freezing, two other considerations prompted him to write the popular article. In a letter to Carl G. Thompson in 1959 he stated:

> You might be interested that I have had more response to the article on FREEZING than to any other article that I have ever written. I am very glad that I wrote that article. It was prompted by two HUSH, HUSH attitudes. One was the attitude by some that it was all mental and the least said about it the better. That is a lot of HOG WASH. The other HUSH was on the part of the archer who was ashamed to let any one know that he had the trouble. To me, this was tragic. It is all so simple. Almost everything that we do is controlled by some of our senses. The eyes play a most prominent part in causing muscular action. This is as it should be but unfortunately in archery it is not a good thing. . . .Unfortunately I was not forewarned and not many others were either so we all got the habit of shooting as soon as the alignment was complete. This is too soon for the best shooting.[32]

D.F. Munro, a Professor of Modern Languages at Kansas State University, was one of the many archers who wrote to Hickman. He stated, "I have just read your article on Freezing, and want to go on record as saying that once again you have put all archers in debt to you. Personally I expect to add many points to my score from now on as a result of reading it."[33]

Max Hamilton, a well-known archer who pioneered in the development of plastic fletching for arrows, wrote to the Editor of *The Archer's Magazine*: "The article on Freezing by Dr. Hickman was the best I have ever read. Especially his analysis of the cause, and his description of the symptoms. I believe that this facet of archery causes more archers to abandon the sport than we realize. . . ."[34] Hickman replied to the Editor, who had forwarded the letter to him: "Thanks for sending Max Hamilton's letter. I have never written an article to which I received better responses. I have given the matter much thought and do feel that I know something about the subject. It makes me happy to hear that my opinions are well received.[35]

Hickman's creative genius was possibly surpassed only by his sense of humor. One example of this dealt with his anti-freeze testing and conclusion. The following anecdote is worth reproducing in full:

ANTI-FREEZE TESTS   February 19, 1948

The results of the first tests of a new anti-freeze gadget were reported in a letter to Paul Klopsteg February 13, 1948. In these tests two variables were changed so that it was deemed advisable to repeat the tests with only one variable. In order to compare the second set of tests with the first ones, the data for both are given.

Test No. 1 - February 11, 1948

An Eastman Kodak pneumatic antenna release such as is used for taking a picture of a group in which the photographer wants to be included was used. The release can be set for intervals of time up to 15 seconds. When it releases it makes a clicking noise which can readily be heard if it is worn on a string around the neck. In the tests, it was set for about 10 seconds. After nocking the arrow (placing it on the string) the catch was released. Plenty of time was available to get well settled on the point and steadied down before it kicked, at which time the arrow was released.

There was just one hitch in these tests, two variables were changed at the same time. In addition to using the pneumatic release as a shooting signal, I had gone up to the Hotel Pennsylvania where I met my brother and had a couple of cocktails.

Results	The Olympic Score was: 60 golds - 90 hits 2 perfect ends and score of 762 *(No rebounds)*
Conclusions	The score was appreciably higher than the average score obtained using other anti-freeze devices. It was therefore concluded that either the new anti-freeze device or the cocktails improved the score.

Test No. 2 - February 18, 1948

In this test the cocktails were omitted, but the new anti-freeze gadget was used.

Results	The Olympic Score was: 65 golds - 90 hits 3 perfect ends with a score of 758. *(There were 7 rebounds)* Had it not been for these rebounds the score would have been 772.
Conclusions	
	1. Since the score of 758 is within 4 points of the previous score of 762, it is concluded that the cocktails did not contribute to the score and that the improvement was due entirely to

the new anti-freeze gadget. As a matter of record, in the test the pneumatic release on one occasion "went off" too quickly, resulting in a 5 (blue). Had this not happened, the score might have been exactly the same as before.

2. Since 7 rebounds occurred in the second test and none in the first, it is concluded that partaking of cocktails eliminates rebounds.[36]

The last archery invention for which Hickman is credited was a Portable Bow Bracing Jig. As bows developed, due to the influence of Hickman and others, the design of the bow switched from predominantly straight limb to recurve. The straight limb bows were fairly easy to brace or string, but due to the re-curved ends, the newer bows were very difficult for archers to hand brace. Most archers placed one leg in between the unstrung bow and string, and used the body and hip as a lever to brace the bow. However, when this method was used, it was very possible to twist the bow limbs. Most manufacturers refused to guarantee the bow if this method of bracing was used. Therefore, a small archer had no recourse but to ask a huskier archer to brace and unbrace his bow. Several bracing jigs had been designed at the time, but none was portable enough to be carried with the archer.[37]

Hickman had been asked by George Crouch, an archer with whom he spent time in Arizona, to work up a design for a good bow bracer. Crouch taught archery to high school girls and spent most of his day bracing and unbracing bows, rather than having to remove the twists that they put into the bow limbs trying to brace them themselves. Hickman wanted a design that could be made simply and used simply. The device he came up with, in a very short time, was instantly well received. He wrote an article for *The Archer's Magazine* including plans to construct the bracer. The accompanying photos show the simple principle. The lower bow limb rests on the bracer and the subject puts her foot on one end of the bracer to hold it steady. The other foot is in a loop of heavy cord that in turn is looped around the handle of the bow. All the archer has to do is lift upward on the upper limb with one hand and attach the loop of the string with the other hand. Hickman included a sentence in the article that made it possible for any individual or manufacturer to freely use the design or a modification of it. (Fig. 72) Earl Hoyt Jr. wrote to Hickman in 1961 and asked if Hoyt Archery Company could build some of Hickman's bracers, with his name on it, and advertise them and sell them in the current catalog.[39] Hickman agreed, specifying that he

103

Fig. 71 Step-through method of
bracing recurve bow[38]

Fig. 72 Hickman Portable
Bow Bracer

wished to receive no royalties from these sales.[40]

In 1966, Chuck Saunders, president of Saunders Archery Company, wrote Hickman inquiring as to the year he had designed the bracer. Saunders had improved the bracer but decided not to patent it due to the work that Hickman had done in the fifties. In his letter he stated:

> I now find that the PAL people (another model of bracer) have a rather recent patent on their design. Ours of course is considerably different, but we know both theirs and ours was antedated by your work in the field.[41]

In his reply to Saunders, he stated: "...of course I did not bother with any patent as I had no desire to commercialize the stringer. Anyone is welcome to use any of the ideas."[42]

No one person did more to analyze archery from a scientific point of view and suggest changes based upon that scientific reasoning than did Hickman. His spark chronograph and shooting machine, new bow designs, investigation of bow backing and development of the process of application, his bow weighing machine and high speed camera, analysis of "Freezing" and development of aids to combat the problem, and his development of the bow bracer, are all testimony to his scientific ingenuity. Hickman's inventive abilities and willingness to share his ideas and designs have truly earned him the title, "Father of Scientific Archery."

REFERENCES

1. Morris Chaklai and Allan Rechtschaffen, "Science Hits the Bull's Eye," *Popular Mechanics Magazine*, 91 (March 1949):175.
2. Clarence N. Hickman, "Velocity and Acceleration of Arrows, Weight and Efficiency of Bows as Affected by Backing of Bow." *Journal of the Franklin Institute*, 208 (October 1929):521.
3. Clarence N. Hickman, "Silk Backing for Bows," (Unpublished, no date). Hickman Archives.
4. Clarence N. Hickman, "Archery Bows," Patent #2285031 United States Patent Office, Washington, D.C., Filed February 21, 1939, Granted June 2, 1942. Hickman Archives.
5. *American Bowman-Review*, 2(August 1941):22.
6. Clarence N. Hickman, *Genealogy of the Hickman Families of Virginia, Kentucky, Indiana and Texas*, (New York: Westminster Printing Company, 1967) p.46.
7. Clarence N. Hickman, Letter to John B. Hibbard, Chairman of NAA Eligibility Committee, July 8, 1961. Hickman Archives.
8. Clarence N. Hickman, Letter to Paul Klopsteg, April 15, 1962, p.3. Hickman Archives.
9. Forrest Nagler, Letter to Clarence N. Hickman, January 22, 1946. Hickman Archives.
10. Clarence N. Hickman, "Fortisan for Backing Bows," *American Bowman-Review*, 15 (March 1946):4.
11. *American Bowman-Review*, 15(March 1946):inside back cover.
12. Hickman, *Genealogy*, p.53.
13. Clarence N. Hickman, "Breaking Strength of Fibers," January 9, 1948 (Unpublished), Hickman Archives.
14. Clarence N. Hickman, "Bow Weighing and Plotting Machine," Arpil 1938 (Unpublished), Hickman Archives.
15. Clarence N. Hickman, Letter to John Mills, April 4, 1940. Hickman Archives.
16. Clarence N. Hickman, "An 8mm Camera with Variable Speeds of From 200 to 6000 Frames per Second," December 8, 1942 (Unpublished), Hickman Archives.
17. Chaklai and Rechtschaffen, "Science Hits the Bull's Eye," p.254.
18. Louis Hochman, *The Complete Archery Book*, (New York:Arco Publishing Company, 1965), p.9.
19. Chaklai and Rechtschaffen, "Science Hits the Bull's Eye," p.254.

20. Patricia Baier, Julia Bowers, Bud Fowkes, Sherwood Schoch, *NAA Instructor's Manual*, 2nd Edition, 1976, p.5.

21. Hickman, "An 8mm Camera..."

22. Clarence N. Hickman, Letter to George Suddell, Eastman Kodak Stores, Inc. September 11, 1946. Hickman Archives.

23. Dr. Robert Elmer, Letter to Clarence N. Hickman, April 20, 1945. Hickman Archives.

24. Horace A. Ford, Esq., "Archery, Its Theory and Practice," *The Field* 6(October 6, 1855):10-15. Hickman Archives.

25. Clarence N. Hickman, "A New Bow Sight," *The American Archer*, (March 1941):7 Hickman Archives.

26. Chaklai and Rechtschaffen, "Science Hits the Bull's Eye," p.254.

27. Hickman, "A New Bow Sight," p.8.

28. Clarence N. Hickman, Letter to Charles Pierson, December 9, 1959. Hickman Archives.

29. Clarence N. Hickman, "Freezing Analyzed," *The Archer's Magazine*, 7(December 1958):9.

30. *Ibid*.

31. *Ibid*., p.10

32. Clarence N. Hickman, Letter to Carl G. Thompson, April 10, 1959. Hickman Archives.

33. D.F. Munro, Professor of Modern Languages, Kansas State University, Letter to Clarence N. Hickman, December 13, 1958. Hickman Archives.

34. Max Hamilton, Letter to J.W. Anderson, Editor, *The Archer's Magazine*, December 27, 1958. Hickman Archives.

35. Clarence N. Hickman, Letter to J.W. Anderson, January 3, 1959. Hickman Archives.

36. Clarence N. Hickman, "Anti-Freeze Tests," February 19, 1948. (Unpublished), Hickman Archives.

37. Clarence N. Hickman, "Portable Bow-Bracing Jig," *The Archer's Magazine*, 7(August 1958):14.

38. Baier, Fowkes, Bowers, Schoch, *NAA Instructor's Manual*, p.27.

39. Earl Hoyt, Jr., Letter to Clarence N. Hickman, May 9, 1961, Hickman Archives.

40. Clarence N. Hickman, Letter to Earl Hoyt, Jr., May 11, 1961, Hickman Archives.

41. Charles N. Saunders, Saunders Archery Company, Letter to Clarence N. Hickman, March 15, 1966. Hickman Archives.

42. Clarence N. Hickman, Letter to Charles Saunders, March 26, 1966, Hickman Archives.

CHAPTER

V

ADMINISTRATIVE CONTRIBUTIONS TO ARCHERY

One might conclude that the highlights of Dr. Hickman's work were theoretical, helping to produce a marked improvement in the archery equipment in use today. He was, though, an archer, who, although his own scores were not outstanding, enjoyed trying out his theories with actual shooting and competing. Since he was a perfectionist in many ways, he never just shot in a tournament, but always volunteered to help in every way possible to make the tournament run smoothly. Hickman joined and organized many archery clubs whose main purpose was to provide tournaments for interested archers. In each organization he spent many hours helping make the sport of archery more pleasant for those who indicated an interest in participating. Dr. Hickman provided leadership which helped archery grow in the New York and Long Island areas, as well as nationally and internationally.

Hickman's first venture into organized archery began in 1926, when he attended the National Archery Association Tournament in Rye, New York as a spectator. He knew some of the members of the Scarsdale Archery Club and soon began shooting with them. He then joined the Metropolitan Archery Association that same year.[1] The first meeting of the Metropolitan Association had been held on October 24, 1925 in New York City. The objectives of the Association were to promote archery in the Metropolitan area, to form archery clubs, and to hold annual meetings of its members for the purpose of competition. All archers residing within 50 miles of City Hall, New York, were eligible for membership. Two tournaments were held annually, one in the spring, and one in the fall, rotating to the sites of different member clubs.

The Metropolitan Archery Association's first tournament was held May 31, 1926, but Hickman did not enter it until three years later. A Metropolitan Round was shot, consisting of 30 arrows each at 100, 80, 60, 50, and 40 yards. Hickman placed 13th of 30 in the Men's Double

Metropolitan Round. This hooked him forever on competition, and he became extremely active in the organization. Hickman was elected Vice-President in 1931 and 1934, and served on the Executive Committee in 1935-36.[2] Besides competing, he helped run tournaments and shared his knowledge with members. He always had his camera on hand to record events, performed magic tricks at meetings, donated prizes for shoots, and brought members up to date on his continuing experiments. In a brief history of the Metropolitan Association written in 1938 by the President, Daniel McKensie, he noted:

> During 1934 and 1935 efforts were made to stimulate interest by dinners, lectures, etc. Special mention deserves to be made of the lecture given by Dr. Hickman in 1934 on the Archer's Paradox, with moving pictures of the flight of an arrow as it leaves the bow.[3]

Hickman shot in every tournament from 1929 on, except during World War II, and in 1950 he was elected President of the Association. During his term as President, he decided to present a gift to each member who attended the Spring Shoot at Bear Mountain, to help celebrate the 25th Anniversary of the club. Since 1926 Hickman had kept his own archives--every notice, set of minutes, and tournament program of the Metropolitan Association. He decided to compile these and write a history of the Association, from 1925 to 1950. This booklet, which numbered 100 pages, was typed by Hickman and reproduced and bound at his expense. Over 350 copies were printed and distributed at no charge. The work included historical highlights, biographical sketches of outstanding leaders and members, list of officers, champions, tournament scores, original and amended constitutions, and autographs of past officers and champions.[4] It was a tremendous task, and could only have been accomplished by Hickman, who had filed everything from the Association over the years. Besides helping to run a superb tournament at Bear Mountain that year, he gave the members and archery in general a valuable token of his love for the sport. (Fig. 73)

The same year that Hickman first entered an archery tournament, 1929, he decided to try to bring together all archers who might be residing near his home in Jackson Heights. He founded the Jackson Heights Archers that same year, and remained President until 1938. The club actively hosted tournaments using a vacant lot donated by the Queensboro Corporation, at Fillmore and Polk Avenues in Jackson Heights. An average of 20 archers per year shot for the club. It was one of the member clubs that hosted tournaments for the Metropolitan Archery Association. In 1932 Hickman was personally instrumental in inviting the

Fig. 73
Metropolitan Archery Association Spring Shoot
Bear Mountain, N.Y. May 14, 1950
Clarence N. Hickman, President

All-Japanese Nippon Archery Club of New York City to join in the Jackson Heights shoots, and in 1935 the club held a novelty shoot for the Nippon Club.[6]

Shortly after he started the Jackson Heights Archers, Hickman realized that the small clubs on Long Island could benefit from an umbrella organization. He sent notices to all archers who lived on Long Island, inviting them to attend a meeting in Rockville Center for the purpose of organizing a Long Island Archery Association. Hickman took charge of the meeting, and a committee was appointed to draw up a constitution. An American and Metropolitan Round were shot, and Hickman placed 4th of 22 men. An informal meet was then held in Rockville Center on May 15, 1932. At this meet Hickman was elected president of the organization. A constitution was adopted and read, in part: "The object of this organization shall be to associate all Archery Clubs and Individual archers on Long Island; to promote common activities and to encourage archery in this area."[7] Hickman, serving as President, was in charge of the first tournament the next fall. (Fig. 74) At this tournament, as an item of interest which was advertised in advance, his Shooting Machine was exhibited and demonstrated on the range each day.[8] Hickman served as Secretary-Treasurer of the club from 1933 through 1937, keeping meticulous records of all activities and sending newsletters. At the end of his term of office, the club had grown to include such clubs as Bowmen of Brth-Ar, Brooklyn Bowmen, Centre Archers, Jackson Heights Archers, New York Archers, North Shore Archers, Rolling Stones Archers, Shinnecock Archers, and Smithtown Archers.[9]

As President of the Long Island Archers, one of Hickman's first actions was to invite the Japanese Archery Club of New York City to attend the first Fall tournament at Jackson Heights. They were also invited to the second tournament at Stony Brook, Long Island, the next year. This then became a custom, and the Japanese were invited to all subsequent Long Island tournaments.[10] As President of the Jackson Heights Archers at the same time, Hickman made sure the Japanese were also invited to the Jackson Heights tournaments.

The cultural exchange, friendships, and goodwill were so impressive as a result of these meets, that Hickman began to conceive of the idea of an International Telegraphic Meet between Japanese and American archers. Working with the Japanese club, Hickman, as Secretary of the Long Island Archers, contacted a club in Japan in 1936. With many letters passing back and forth between Japan and the United States, an agreement was finally worked out.[11] Hickman was able to get the National Archery Association to agree to the meet and officially sponsor it.[12] The tournament in the United States was held at Holmes Airport,

Finsbury Archers Ticket
About 1676

37th Ave., (Polk Ave.) and 84th Street

Jackson Heights

Long Island, New York

Fig. 74

Jackson Heights, N.Y., October 17, 1937. No bowsights were permitted, and the Americans shot 30 arrows at 40 yards at a 48" target, and 30 arrows at 31 yards at a 14½" target resting on the ground (Japanese Round).[13] The Japanese, who shot at the American School in Tokyo, were rained out on October 17, and shot on October 24. They again experienced bad weather, and shot only the American Round. There were 30 competitors in each country, but Japan selected the representatives based on tryouts, while the United States basically took members of the Long Island Archers who wished to compete. The Japanese won this contest, with an average score of 195.03 to the Americans's score of 163.8. It must be noted that at this time the Japanese did not use bowsights as part of their shooting technique, while the Americans did. Therefore, the Americans were greatly penalized by having to remove the bowsights from their bows for the competition. Pictures were taken in Japan and an album mailed to officials in the United States, with additional albums able to be purchased by competitors.[14] Commemorative medals were struck by the Japanese and sent to all participants (Fig. 76). The tournaments received good coverage in the local papers, and all decided that the event would contribute to the overall appeal of archery. It was decided at this time to hold a second telegraphic meet the following year, with some change in the rules. After lengthy correspondence, the Americans were allowed to compete with bowsights and only the American round became official.[15] In the second tournament, shot September 25 and October 1, 1938, only days before Canton and Hankow, China fell to the Japanese, the Americans defeated the Japanese, with an average score of 153.5 to 151.2. (Appendix F, G, H) (Fig. 75 to 85) No other international contests were held until after World War II.

It is an irony of the times that Dr. Hickman, who was made the first honorary member of the Nippon Archery Club in 1935, and who did so much to foster good will between the Japanese and the United States, would find himself unable to help the president of the Nippon Club in 1943. In August of 1943, Hickman received a letter from the U.S. Department of Justice regarding Tatsugoro Okajima and his status as an Alien Enemy. (Appendix I) Hickman, who was in Washington at the time, and heavily involved in war activities, was unable to act as a sponsor for Mr. Okajima. It was only long after the war that Dr. Hickman was able to resume his friendships and shooting with the Japanese club. His initial efforts on behalf of International Archery Meets were well received by the National Archery Association, and were the first of thousands of invitational meets in the years to come.

Besides starting the Jackson Heights and Long Island Archery Associations, Hickman was also responsible for organizing the Bell Telephone Archery Club in 1932. The club consisted of about 15 members, who shot at the Robin Hood Range in Newark, N.J. (Fig. 86) Since at that time only the New York Bell Labs were participating, the trip to Newark (the only range available) resulted in members gradually losing interest. In 1938, after sporadic attendance, Hickman reorganized the club and was able to obtain a range at 795 Broadway in Manhattan. At the same time, he organized clubs at the Murray Hill and Whippany Bell Labs in New Jersey, where facilities were found for shooting on the premises or at local clubs in New Jersey. (Fig. 87) An average of 50 archers remained active in the combined Bell Labs clubs until the war. At that time the Manhattan range was lost, and shooting was discontinued. On October 17, 1946, the club was reorganized, and about 30 archers shot in the basement of Washington Irving High School in New York. Although he was active in many other clubs, and was busy with his work,

Fig. 75 1937 Japanese-American Telegraphic Meet.
Mr. H.C. Amos. Principal of the American School of Tokyo
Mr. D. McAlpin Pyle. Honorary Attache of U.S. Embassy
in Tokyo.
Mr. Matskichi Koyama, President of Kyushinkai.

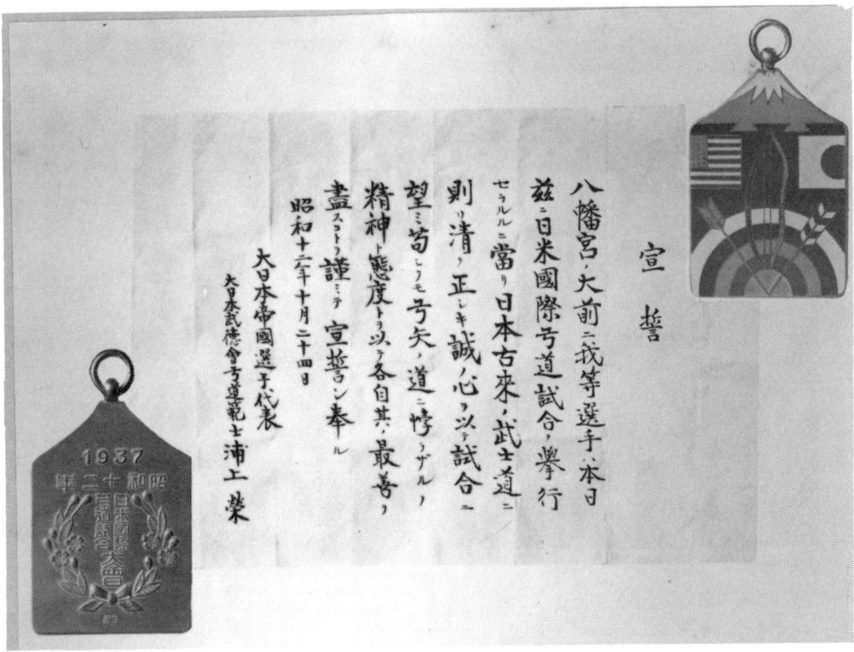

Fig. 76 International Badge and Oath for all contestants.

Fig. 77 Devotion Services in front of Archery Shrine.

Fig. 78 The Contest at 40 Yards.

Fig. 79 Hanshi -
Mr. Sakaye Uragami,
Front

Fig. 80 Views of Front and Back Members during the Contest.

117

Fig. 81
Tournament Officials - Left To Right - Standing: W. H. Jackson,
Dr. R.P. Elmer, Mr. S. Mizutani, Mr. H. Matsuo.
Seated: G. A. Smith, E. Derwood Myers, Mr. K. Tanaka,
C. N. Hickman.

Fig. 82

American Archers

Fig. 83

Archers - Target No. 4 - Left To Right Dr. Robert P. Elmer, Walter Miller, Claude Johnson, Lester Rexon, W. H. Jackson

Fig. 84

High Scoring Archers
Left To Right:
1st Harry Gage - 50 Yd.
Score - 30 -- 210
2nd C.J. Weese - 50 yd.
Score - 30 -- 200
3rd Proctor Wetherill -
50 Yd.
Score -30 -- 196

Fig. 85   Japanese Target

Fig. 86   1932 Bell Telephone Archery Club Robin Hood Range Newark, N.J.

Hickman spent much time recruiting archers at the three Bell Labs sights. He organized contests and contributed prizes for the contests between the Laboratories. He edited various archery bulletins in which meet scores were included and sent to all members. He formulated a handicap system, which allowed archers to compete together more fairly. He was continually bringing in guest speakers and outstanding archery figures for demonstrations and did much to stimulate interest in the sport.[17] One of his most notable attempts was his production of an Archery Hour show, which was advertised for six weeks at the Bell Labs, with notices, reminders, and displays in the display cases each week. (Fig. 88) The Hour was most notable for Hickman's re-enactment of the William Tell episode.

Always a showman and master of illusion, Hickman had worked out a safe way to do the trick using a live volunteer. Hickman asked Helen Smith, Secretary of the Club to volunteer as the "victim." After placing the apple on her head and getting ready to shoot, Hickman complained that he could not concentrate on the apple because of her pretty face and nice dress. He then placed a large black cloth over her. He was assisted by another member, who had come to the demonstration dressed as a nurse with a large first aid kit in prominent view. He placed the apple on Mrs.

Smith's covered head, and asked if she had any last requests. She answered, "Yes, don't miss the apple." He then asked that some soft music be played. With the strains of Chopin's Funeral March as a musical background, he sent an arrow straight through the apple. (Fig. 89) As written up in the Bell Laboratories Record of December 1949:

> Then he slowly removed the cloth and, as it was being lowered, it was observed that her hair had turned white. Remarking that she had evidently been badly frightened, he lowered the cloth still further, and those who were alert noted that Mrs. Smith was sitting in the box instead of on it, and that the lid of the box had been raised and acted as a shield. A cross member had also been raised which concealed a false head and shoulders. Pretending that he had revealed the trick by accident, he quickly raised the cloth and when lowered again she was again sitting on the box, the dummy having been folded down so that it was inside the box. The audience was delighted with the program and about twenty new members have been recruited for the Club. [19]

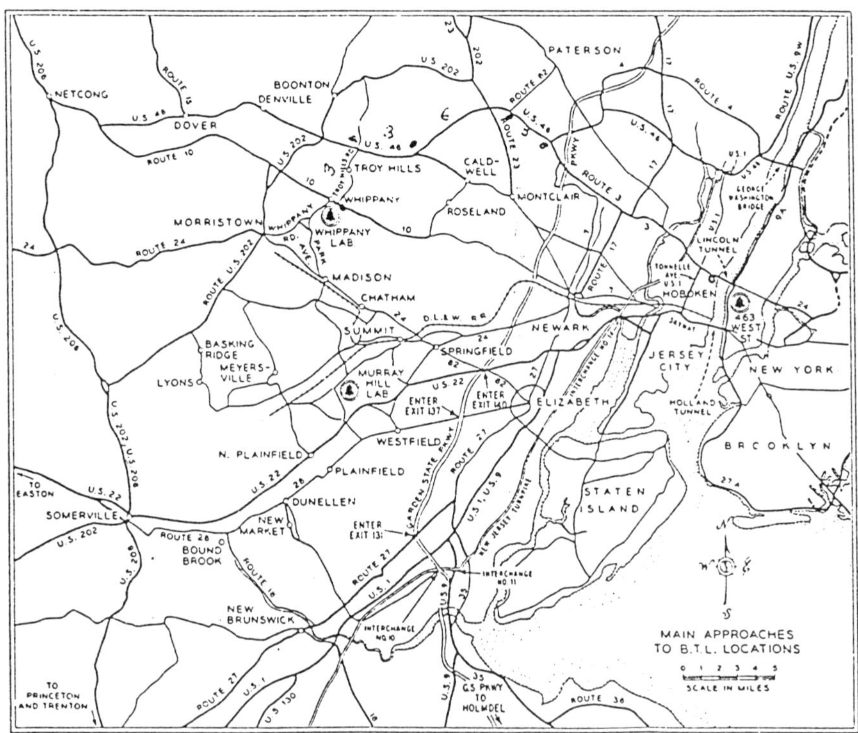

Fig. 87   Map Locations of Bell Telephone Laboratories, 1932

In appreciation for his contribution to the sport of archery and his efforts at Bell Labs, the Bell Archers gave Hickman a luncheon and trophy, (Fig. 90) with the bow of the trophy being a replica of his new bow of radical design. [20] (Fig. 91) Shortly before he was to retire in January 1950, after 20 years with Bell Telephone, the Club again gave him a surprise party and many nice gifts. Hickman produced a small booklet of appreciation for each of the members, and included a personal note and photograph of himself at full draw with one of his new true center shot bows. (Fig. 92) It was through Hickman's efforts alone that the three branches of the Bell Labs Archery Clubs continued to shoot from 1932 through 1950 and beyond. He returned many times after his retirement to shoot in the Bell tournaments.

Another organization in which Hickman held membership was the Eastern Archery Association. This association was founded in 1879 and provided for interstate competition for member clubs in states from Maine to Virginia. Hickman joined the organization in 1927, shooting in all the tournaments, which were usually held in June or July. In 1954, he served as Delegate-at-Large, and the next year he was elected President of the organization. Again wanting to make a special donation to the ar-

Fig. 88   The Archery Hour Display

Fig. 89   Hickman's "William Tell Shot"

chers, he compiled a book of poems written by an early archer and leader
of the period, James Duff (1870-1935). [21] Duff was one of the early
founders of the Metropolitan Archery Association, and Hickman
dedicated the History of the Metropolitan Archery Association booklet,
written in 1950, to his memory. He then worked with Duff's widow and
daughter to find and reproduce all of James Duff's poems in a commem-
morative booklet.[22] James Duff had been instrumental in re-organizing
the Eastern Archery Association after World War I, becoming its president in 1923 and later an Honorary Member. Hickman again researched
and organized the entire collection of poems, presenting each member
with a copy at the 77th Anniversary Tournament, held July 3-7, 1956 at
Springfield College. [23] Once again, Hickman was not content to serve only as president of a large organization, but put forth the effort to provide
that extra something for the benefit of the archers.

Although Hickman did not serve in the New York Archery Club as
an officer, he did lend his support in many other ways. In 1938, Myrtle
and Edward B. Miller organized the New York Archers Club. The purpose of this club was to try to provide archery ranges in Queens, Staten
Island, the Bronx, New York City, Long Island, and Westchester.
Hickman served on the Advisory Board from the club's inception until

1950. In an attempt to help attract members, he was often the speaker at meetings, showing his Archer's Paradox film, films of the Japanese archery contests, taking pictures of members competing and giving them copies of the photographs, performing his William Tell trick, and serving as Master of Ceremonies at archery demonstrations. He also served as Field Captain for tournaments and provided trophies for the New York Archers inter-club meets. Through the Millers' efforts and Dr. Hickman's help, the New York Archers became one of the largest clubs in the United States at that time, with a membership of approximately 200 archers.[24]

Fig. 90   Trophy for outstanding achievements in the science and practice of archery being awarded by W.G. Laskey to C.N. Hickman at B.T.L. Archery Club Luncheon, March 4, 1948. Seated at Mr. Laskey's left is Mrs. Myrtle K. Miller.

Hickman was extremely impressed by the Miller's enthusiasm for the sport and their dedication to helping archery grow. He was even more impressed by their efforts to turn Teela-Wooket Archery Camp of Roxbury, Vermont into an outstanding educational institution. Before 1937, it seemed that archers, archery instructors, and coaches were on their own. Archery had often been a part of the physical education curriculum in schools, but the instruction left much to be desired. There were no

Fig. 91

Awarded March 4, 1948
to C.N. Hickman

Fig. 92   Centerfold of Hickman's thank you booklet to
Bell Archery Club members.

special schools for archery training until the Miller's conceived of the idea and started Teela-Wooket Archery Camp in 1937 in Roxbury, Vermont.[25] Dr. Hickman, impressed by the course content and ideals of the school, took the course in 1938, along with 26 other students. He was so impressed with TWAC, and the Millers were so impressed with him, that Hickman agreed to become Dean of the school. (Fig. 93) He faithfully attended every year, insisting it be at his own expense, contributing in the areas of science and equipment design and maintenance, as well as basic archery instruction. He was so faithful to his voluntary teaching responsibilities that in a letter to William Jackson of Robin Hood Archery Company, he stated:

> I am looking forward to an interesting archery season. Unfortunately, I cannot attend the Eastern this year because to do so would mean that I would have to disappoint Myrtle Miller. I feel that the work she is doing is sufficiently important not to give her too much discouragement. She has operated this camp for many years at a loss. [26]

Hickman allowed his picture to appear on the TWAC advertising brochure and attempted to promote the school through his contacts in the various clubs. (Fig. 94) In 1948 the staff at TWAC, who were primarily volunteer professional educators, voted to confer upon Hickman the title Doctor of Archery. (Fig. 95) Since this was and continues to be the only archery educational institution in the world, it is the only one that can grant this title. In 1955, in a personal letter to Dr. Hickman, Mrs. Miller wrote:

> It'd be impossible to try to put into words the way Eddie and I feel about you and your great loyalty to TWAC, but we wish you could know through vibrations, extra sensory perception or some way exactly how very much we appreciate it all. Really, had it not been for your constant support, enthusiasm, interest, and encouragement, these past years could have been much more difficult than they were. But, somehow every time things seemed to get really tough. . .we'd think about our wonderful Dean. It just seemed knowing you were so completely back of us made the load much lighter and we do hope you know how very much we appreciate it all. . . .[27]

Teela-Wooket Archery Camp, known as The World Archery Center since 1976, is now located in the Pocono Mountains of Pennsylvania. It celebrated its 45th Anniversary in 1982. Dr. Hickman died just one month before the 1981 session, which he was planning to attend.

Fig. 93   C.N. Hickman -- TWAC DEAN (1950)

Fig. 94   Teela-Wooket Archery Camp Brochure, June 1949

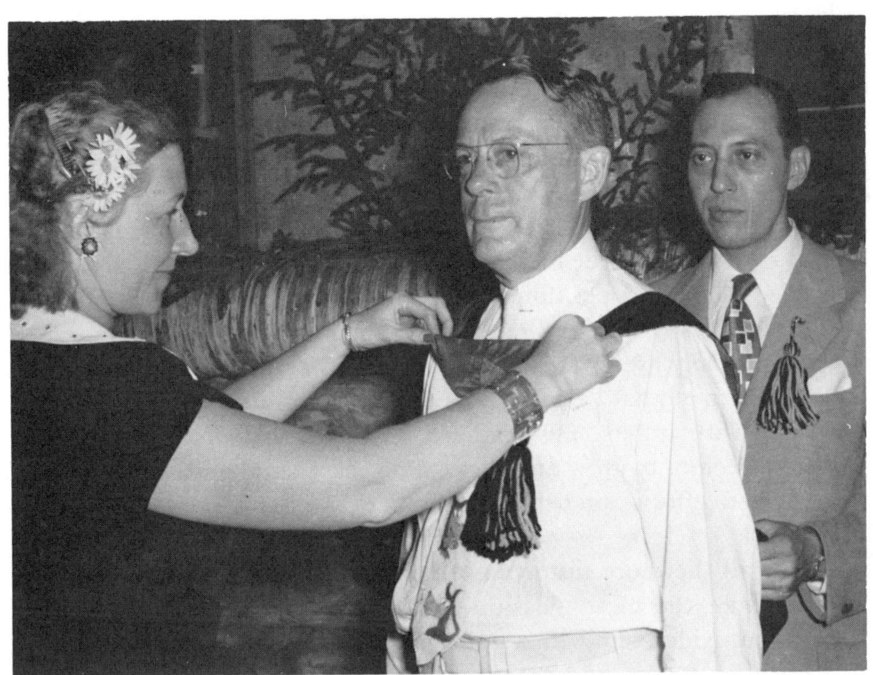

Fig. 95   Doctor of Archery

During the 40th Anniversary session, he again brought down the house with his magic tricks, demonstration of his various inventions, films of the Archer's Paradox, and his humorous remarks. Although he had turned from a career in teaching to one as a researcher, his love of teaching made TWAC the one archery enterprise to which he dedicated himself until the end of his life.

From the beginning of his interest in organized archery (1929), he started an archery book collection, compiling one of the world's largest and most valuable libraries of archery books, many of them rare, and complete volumes of British and American archery journals. He carefully catalogued his collection, which includes a copy of *Toxophilus*, by Roger Ascham, the second edition, printed in 1571. In June 1967, Hickman donated the entire collection, valued at that time at over $5,000, to the Lilly Library, Indiana University, Bloomington, Indiana. [28]

Through the years Hickman donated his administrative talents and inspirational character to many archery organizations. He was made an Honorary Member of all organizations and received numerous awards and recognition for his service (See Appendix L). It is interesting to note the length of time Hickman served as secretary of so many organizations.

He had a penchant for collecting and organizing every possible bit of information about each club, which put him in the position of being extremely knowledgeable about all aspects of each organization. It would lead one to suspect that Hickman may have preferred the position of secretary to that of the presidency. The possession of all data relating to the history of the organization, membership, decisions, and minutes, certainly provided him with the opportunity to make recommendations to those in authority and the membership at large, relative to any issue. His knowledge gave him a position of power and quiet control. This, coupled with his limitless energy and enthusiasm, enabled him to accomplish so much in so many areas. Hickman's interest in archery was such that he wished to learn all that he could about all phases of it and then share that knowledge with others. His leadership efforts on behalf of the sport enabled new clubs to grow and the established ones to grow stronger. His multi-faceted efforts on behalf of archery, will not soon, if ever, be duplicated.

It is all the more disturbing then, to realize that the sport which gave Hickman the most pleasure and outlet for his creative energies, ultimately provided him with a most painful experience during his retirement years.

References

1. Helene Huck, "Dr. Clarence N. Hickman--His Contribution to Archery," *The Archer's Magazine*, 3(October 1954):3-5.
2. Clarence N. Hickman, "Metropolitan Archery Association--Programs, Clippings, Scores, Correspondence, 1928," Hickman Archives.
3. Daniel McKensie, "Brief History of the Metropolitan Archery Association," 1938 (Unpublished), Hickman Archives.
4. Clarence N. Hickman, *Metropolitan Archery Association History, 1925-1950*, Privately Printed, Hickman Archives.
5. Clarence N. Hickman, "Metropolitan Archery Association--Silver Anniversary Year," 1950, Hickman Archives.
6. C.N. Hickman, "Jackson Heights Archers--1928-1941," Hickman Archives.
7. Clarence N. Hickman, "Long Island Archers--Tournaments, Correspondence Notices," 1931-1941, Hickman Archives.
8. Long Island Archers Fall Tournament Program, October 15-16, 1931, Hickman Archives.

9. *Ibid.*

10. *Ibid.*

11. S. Itoh, Yokohama, Japan, Letter to Clarence N. Hickman, May 23, 1937, Hickman Archives.

12. Paul Klopsteg, NAA Board of Governors, Letter to Clarence N. Hickman, September 7, 1937, Hickman Archives.

13. Clarence Hickman, "Japanese-American Archery Contest Rules," October 1937, Hickman Archives.

14. Memorial Album of Japanese American Archery Tournament, Tokyo, Japan, October 24, 1937, Hickman Archives.

15. Clarence N. Hickman, "Japanese-American Archery Tournament, Tokyo Japan," October 24, 1937, Hickman Archives.

16. Clarence Hickman, Photos of Japanese American Archery Contest, Jackson Heights, N.Y., 1938, Hickman Archives.

17. Clarence Hickman, "Bell Telephone Laboratories Club, 1932-1950," Hickman Archives.

18. Clarence N. Hickman, "Photos and Archery Hour Information-- Bell Laboratories File," 1932-1950, Hickman Archives.

19. "The Archery Hour," *Bell Laboratories Record*, (December 1949):460, Hickman Archives.

20. Clarence N. Hickman, "Bell Telephone Laboratories Archery Club, 1932-1950," Hickman Archives.

21. Clarence N. Hickman, "Eastern Archery Association, 1937-1956," Hickman Archives.

22. Clarence N. Hickman, Editor, *Archery Poems* by James Duff and May Duff Murray, Privately Printed, 1956, Hickman Archives.

23. Eastern Archery Association, 77th Anniversary Tournament Results, July 3-7, 1956, Springfield College, Springfield, Massachusetts, Hickman Archives.

24. Clarence N. Hickman, "New York Archers--Notices, Correspondence, Point-of-Aim," Beginning May 1938, Hickman Archives.

25. Charlie Krich, "TWAC's 40th Anniversary," *Archery World* (July 1977):22. Hickman Archives.

26. Clarence N. Hickman, Letter to W.H. Jackson, Robin Hood Archery Company, N.J., March 8, 1949, Hickman Archives.

27. Myrtle K. Miller, Letter to Clarence Hickman, September 22, 1955, Hickman Archives.

28. "Book Collection Donated to Library," Bloomington Tribune, Bloomington, Indiana, January 14, 1968.

CHAPTER

VI

CLARENCE HICKMAN:
AMATEUR OR PROFESSIONAL?

"I am sorry to tell you," Hickman wrote to his friend and member of the Board of Governors of the National Archery Association, "that you will not see me at the Eastern, the National, or any other tournament. I am through with organized archery," he told Dr. Paul Crouch. "I am not even going to TWAC...." [1] This startling statment made in early 1962 by the man who had done so much to influence the sport of archery over the previous 35 years, came as a result of changes that had occurred within the National Archery Association in 1961. Dr. Hickman was so upset by these changes regarding his amateur status, and the manner in which they were brought about, that he dropped completely out of the archery scene from 1962 through 1975.

The National Archery Association (NAA), the governing body of archery in the United States, had periodically considered making a distinction between amateur and non-amateur. This was not deemed necessary until 1952, when the United States became involved in organized international competition, and it became necessary to abide by FITA rules, or rules dictated by the Federation of International Target Archers. The NAA conformed to the FITA rules by adopting its own definition of amateur, which allowed a person to make 20% of his earnings in archery and still be considered an amateur. [2]

In 1960 it appeared imminent that archery would be added to the Olympic Games in Japan in 1964. In order to qualify for the Olympics, the NAA had to become part of the United States Olympic Association and abide by even more strict rules. A committee was formed in 1960 within the NAA to investigate the set of rules necessary to meet Olympic standards. The rules, which follow, were presented and approved by the Board of Governors early the following year.

133

REGULATIONS GOVERNING AMATEUR COMPETITION

Approved January 21, 1961
National Archery Association of the U. S.

An amateur archer is one who engages in archery solely for the pleasure and physical, mental or social benefits he derives therefrom and to whom archery is nothing more than an avocation.

1. PRIZES - The amateur archer may not compete for cash prizes in any sum, nor may he compete for trophies or awards suitably inscribed of any kind worth more than $70.00 for first prize. $40.00 for second place, and $20.00 for third prize.

2. EXHIBITIONS - The amateur archer may not exhibit his skill as an archer for pay.

3. INSTRUCTING - The amateur archer may not accept pay for instructing or coaching in archery. Any school and college teacher, including physical education teachers, whose work is solely educational and who are not paid, directly or indirectly, for coaching of archery for competition, are eligible amateurs.

4. ENDORSEMENT - The amateur archer may not permit his name or picture to be used in print, over television, radio or other public communication system in an advertisement or in the endorsement of any company or product. The use of an archer's photograph in news media or the participation in radio broadcast or telecast is not prohibited, provided the archer receives no compensation of any kind, directly or indirectly, in connection with the use of such photograph or such participation.

5. EXPENSES - The maximum expenses which an amateur archer may request, receive or accept in connection with his competition or participation in any event, exhibition or tournament, shall not exceed (a) his actual expenditures for travel up to the cost of first class public transportation fare, including the cost of such transportation to and from airport or railroad terminal: and (b) his actual expenditures for maintenance, including lodging, and meals, up to a total of fifteen ($15) dollars per day for each day during the time occupied between going to and returning from the event, exclusive of necessary travel time. The period for which such expenses may be allowed shall not exceed one (1) day after the event unless for good reason a longer period is expressly approved by the Qualifications Committee: (c) vouchers or receipts evidencing payment of actual expenditures for transportation and lodging shall be furnished by the archer and attached to the expense statement to be submitted to the Qualifications Committee.

6. EMPLOYMENT BY A FIRM
The amateur archer may not accept money from a firm or individual engaged in some phase of archery promotion without regularly being on the payroll and work at a specific job in that organization. If he is employed by an archery manufacturer or sales firm, he may not receive paid time off during the normal work week (35 hours) for the practice of archery and may not have his expenses paid in any way by the firm in which he is employed. The above will not preclude attending a tournament during the normal two-week paid vacation period available to most people.

7. SELF-EMPLOYMENT - The amateur archer if self-employed in the manufacture of archery tackle must not use his shooting prowess or his name or photograph as a basis for selling his wares.

8. AMATEUR COMPETITION WITH A NON-AMATEUR - The amateur archer may participate in competition with the non-amateur only where the tournament entries are confined to the bona fide members of a club. The amateur may not compete with the non-amateur at the state, regional, or national level. He may shoot on the same field, under the same tournament management, in the same tournament, but must compete in a different division from the non-amateur; that is, he may not compete with the non-amateur for the same awards or prizes.

9. EFFECTIVE DATE - The effective date of these regulations is March 15, 1961.[4]

The Board also adopted a retroactivity rule which stated:

> The NAA accepts as amateur, from January 1, 1958 to March 15, 1961 any archer who has not received a cash prize in excess of $70 or who has not been paid (other than expenses) for putting on archery exhibitions.[3]

By July 1961, the amateur competition rules had been widely distributed and were known to most members. At the Eastern Archery Tournament, held at Springfield College, Mass., July 4-8, 1961, Dr. Hickman received a jolt. Several archers told him that, according to the rules as they were printed, they did not think he would pass as an amateur. As a man who had spent so much time serving the sport, giving freely of his time and personal money, this hurt him terribly. The day he returned from the Easterns, Hickman wrote a letter to John Hibbard, a member of the Board of Governors of the National Archery Association. Hickman asked about the professional or amateur status of a person in 19 different hypothetical situations. He received a reply from Hibbard on July 20, 1961, stating that he would try to answer the questions, but that they would not be official rulings, as rules interpretations must be made by the Chairman, who at that time was Marvin Schmidt. Of the 19 different situations, most were classified as amateurs. However, in several situations, the amateur status was not clearly defined. One of Hickman's questions concerned a person, such as himself, who edited and sold a book on archery. Hibbard's answer: "I would definitely want more information as to the character of the book and status of the archer; but in most cases that type of activity would disqualify an archer as an amateur.[5] Another question related to a person whose name was used in advertisements of an archery school, such as a Dean, Staff member, or consultant. Hibbard answered that he was not sure that he had thought through this question, but would probably accept the person as an amateur. Hickman asked a question about a technical man who received no payments but whose name was used in connection with advertising an archery product. Hibbard said he would lean toward accepting the case as permissable for an amateur, but not without more specifics. Another sample question concerned an archer who was paid to appear on TV and shoot an arrow tipped with a watch, to demonstrate that the watch would withstand the impact. Hibbard stated that such an action would be disqualifying, in his view. Hibbard further stated:

> While I am not qualified to speak for the Board of Governors of the National Archery Association, it is my definite understanding

that the NAA intends to apply no disqualifying tests retroactively
except those which under the rules of the AAU are permanently
disqualifying. In general I believe we may say that in a question of
eligibility for the Olympics, the fact of having won money in competition or of having given demonstrations for pay would be disqualifying, regardless of when it occurred. I think it equally sure
that infractions of the rest of the rules, occurring before March
15, 1961, will not be disqualifying.[6]

Hickman was very disturbed by Hibbard's letter. First, he did not
feel that it adequately answered all his questions. Second, he was livid
about the retroactive clause. Hickman stated that he and others had been
told that since there had never been a professional class in the sport, that
every archer would have the opportunity to choose the class he wished to
join. He was shocked to learn that many archers were being denied or
would be denied amateur status because at some time in the past they had
violated some rule that did not exist at the time of the violation. In his
own case, Hickman stated:

When I attended the Eastern Archery Tournament I learned that
there were many rules that would keep real amateur archers from
being so classified. In my own case I was told by several archers
that if I were ever challenged, that I would be classed as a professional. They pointed out several rules that would make it impossible for me to retain amateur standing. There was no intimation
that I would be challenged but the mere fact that they felt as they
did made me so sick at heart that I do not see how I can ever get
the joy out of the sport that I have had for so many years.[7]

Hickman had friends at Bell Labs who had agreed to do a Timex
commercial, taping watches on to arrows and shooting them. According
to the retroactive rules, these two archers were pros because they accepted
money above and beyond expenses to do this one time show. Hickman
commented:

. . .Each appeared on a Timex show and were paid and according
to Hibbard they are now professional archers although such an
organization did not exist at the time they appeared on the show
and no such thing was in the offering. To me, this is disgusting.
The lads are no more professional than I am. . . .Why should they
spend all that time in rehearsal, etc., for an advertising concern
without pay. They have always given their free time to archery
clubs, etc. They do not even know that they are professional and I
am not telling them.[8]

Hickman was also bitter about the fact that his friend, Ann Weber

Hoyt, leading woman archer in the United States at the time, was classified as a professional, according to the retroactive clause. Within the time frame cited, 1958-61, Ann had shot in a money shoot. She had been advised by a member of the NAA Board of Governors that she could do this, and she later donated the money to a scholarship fund. However, she was denied amateur status and was therefore ineligible for international competition.[9]

Hickman wrote back to John Hibbard on September 10, 1961, stating that he was not satisfied by several of the answers to his questions. By this time, Hibbard had become the Chairman of the Rules Committee. Hickman wrote a five page letter in which he outlined all his archery activities and contributions and requested a definite ruling on his status. He sent copies to President Clayton Shenk, and Marvin Schmidt, Ray Gooley, and Dr. Oxnam, all members of the NAA Board of Governors. Hickman was upset with the actions of his fellow archers and stated that he should only be classified as an amateur. There was doubt in his own mind, though, and he had taken much time to compose the lengthy letter. He did not receive an answer from John Hibbard for over a month, and he received no replies whatever from the persons to whom he had sent copies. This long wait completely devastated Hickman. When Hibbard's reply finally came, Hickman had already washed his hands of the sport. Just before the Eastern Archery Tournament the following year, Hickman wrote a note to the Secretary of the organization in which he stated:

> The manner in which the NAA rushed into professional archery classifications and made the drastic rules retroactive, killed my enthusiasm for archery. I had hoped that archery would add greatly to my pleasure and span of life. Now I find that the reverse is true. It seemed only fair that I should let you know why I have dropped out of all archery activities.[10]

Although the Board of Governors of the NAA had assured Hickman that he was not a professional, he remained so bitter about the way in which the amateur situation was handled that he did not shoot or participate in archery for the next 13 years. The timing of this entire incident was most unfortunate, as Hickman's wife became very ill in 1962. He spent three years caring for her in very trying circumstances. He could have benefited greatly from his archery friends and activities during this time, but had little of it to use for support.

For years the Millers had tried to convice Hickman to come back to The World Archery Center, where his expertise was valued and needed. Finally, in 1976, the year the Center moved from Vermont to Pennsylvania, Hickman agreed to return. It is suspected that he did this solely to please the Millers, and not because he suddenly lost the bitterness within him. His experiences at the Center were so gratifying that he agreed while there to return again the following year.

In 1977, at the age of 87, Hickman was inducted into both the National Archery Association Hall of Fame and the New York State Archery Association Hall of Fame. Both organizations recognized the magnitude of Hickman's contribution to the sport, and his acceptance signified that he had begun to make peace within himself and accept the changes that had occurred through the years within the sport. Hickman's only real archery activities after that were updating his personal archery files and looking forward to returning to The World Archery Center each year. His death in May of 1981, one month short of returning to the Center, marked the end of nearly five decades of personal contributions to the sport of archery and the people involved in it. Hickman's life and contributions were unique. No one person did so much in such a short time to take the sport of archery from the stone age to the space age.

Fig. 96   Ann Weber Hoyt Presenting NAA Hall of Fame Plaque to Clarence Hickman, 1977

REFERENCES

1. Clarence N. Hickman, Letter to Paul Crouch, April 14, 1962, Hickman Archives.
2. "A Brief Clarification of Pertinent Subjects for Amateur Archery Competition," *National Archery Association*, Chicago, ILL., July 24, 1961, Hickman Archives.
3. Robert Rhode, History of the National Archery Association 1946-1978, Volume II, (Michigan: McNaughton and Gum, 1974), p.948.
4. "Regulations Governing Amateur Competition," National Archery Association approved January 21, 1961, Hickman Archives.
5. John Hibbard, Letter to Clarence N. Hickman, July 20, 1961, p.2, Hickman Archives.
6. *Ibid.*, p.3.
7. Clarence N. Hickman, Letter to John Hibbard, Harrisburg, Pa., September 10, 1961, Hickman Archives.
8. Clarence N. Hickman, Letter to Paul Crouch, April 14, 1962, Hickman Archives.
9. Interviews with Ann Weber Hoyt, May 1980, October 1982
10. Clarence N. Hickman, Letter to Mrs. Ruth Dick, Secretary, Eastern Archery Association, June 14, 1962, Hickman Archives.
11. Clarence N. Hickman, Letter to John Hibbard, September 10, 1961, p.3, Hickman Archives.

APPENDIX

Appendix A

Fig. 97 Cover of program used by C.N. Hickman in 1911 and 1912. Hickman Archives

Appendix B

The figure reproduces the inside of a program. Its text reads:

=ANNOUNCEMENT=

We are glad to introduce to the public Mr. Clarence N. Hickman, the Hoosier Magician and Entertainer, He has appeared in Public many times and has always met with complete success and in his home town he has a "packed house" whenever he chooses in spite of the generally believed idea that a prophet is without honor among his own people.

Mr. Hickman is a cultured and refined gentleman having a wide range of experience. He gives a full evening entertainment and his program from start to finish is full of fun and mystery

Mr. Hickman wishes to call the attention of the Public to the fact that his programme is entirely original. He presents a number of unexcelled stage illusions that baffle the wisest and amuse all. In connection with the experiments in magic, Mr. Hickman introduces comedian work of the most comical nature, thus giving one big act of mirth and mystery. Satisfaction guaranteed or money refunded.

All who enjoy seeing a high grade entertainment should not fail to see Prof. Hickman, who is presenting an excellent programme of music and magic comedy. Mr. Hickman, is the only magician presenting large stage illusions in the smaller cities. His experiments are entirely original and unexcelled. The comedian will keep you laughing from start to finish with his comical original pranks. A refined entertainment is guaranteed.

I have known Mr. Hickman since childhood and have been associated with him in business for several years. As a magician he is original and unexcelled. His cabinet trick alone is worth the price of admission.
S. M. HENDRICKS, Clothier,
Waynetown, Ind.

I am personally acquainted with Mr. Hickman, the Magician and Entertainer. He is a member of my church and I have been associated with him for some time. He is a cultured and refined young man holding the confidence of the entire town. As an entertainer, Mr. Hickman is a genius. One characteristic he has is originality, patterning after no other magician but presenting a programme equally as good.
JOHN G. BENSON,
Waynetown, Ind.

Fig. 98   Inside of program used by C.N. Hickman for magic performances. Hickman Archives

Appendix C

T = Telephone (31)
A = Archery (2)
R = Rockets (37)
P = Piano (2)
M = Mines (2)

	Issue Date	File Date	Serial No.	Patent No.	Subject
M	6-30-25	5-17-24	714,099	1,543,920	Self Calibrating Drifting Mine
P	4-14-31	6-4-27	196,414	1,800,796	Player Piano Valve Unit
P	9-15-31	7-25-28	295,258	1,823,142	Grand Piano Action
T	1-23-34	4-15-31	530,167	1,944,238	Telegraphone Tape Recorder
T	12-4-34	9-13-33	689,194	1,982,810	Magnetic Material Pole Pieces
P	7-12-36	5-1-29	359,466	1,866,707	Piano Key Action
T	6-4-35	4-15-31	530,168	2,003,968	Magnetic Telegraphone System
T	7-2-35	3-31-32	602,186	2,006,455	Telegraphic Message Recording System
T	7-6-37	10-7-36	104,384	2,086,130	Telegraphone Telephone Recorder
T	10-26-37	9-18-35	41,013	2,096,805	Phonographic Tape Recorder
T	11-30-37	6-22-35	27,890	2,100,317	Bow, Radical Design
T	1-25-38	3-27-36	71,102	2,108350	Testing System for Magnetic Tape
T	6-14-38	8-18-36	96,573	2,120,408	Selective Switch Crossbar
T	1-24-38	8-6-36	94,527	2,144,844	Magnetic Telegraphone Disc Type
T	6-27-39	8-4-38	222,974	2,164,034	Selector Switch Tape Switch
T	1-2-40	2-21-36	65,020	2,185,300	Telegraphone Pole Pieces
T	1-2-40	11-13-36	110,622	2,185,374	Selective Switch Pneumatic
T	1-30-40	6-21-38	214,913	2,188,659	Selector Switch Brush for Tape Switch
T	8-27-40	12-9-39	308,497	2,212,830	Relay Magnetic
T	4-29-41	7-9-38	218,335	2,240,039	Selector Switch Pneumatic
T	5-19-42	6-4-41	396,520	2,283,366	Line and Cut-Off Relay
A	6-2-42	2-21-39	257,650	2,285,031	Archery Bow, Backing
T	6-9-42	12-26-40	371,672	2,285,657	Brush Carriage For Tape Selector Switch
T	8-25-42	11-27-40	367,338	2,293,823	Multicontact Relay
T	11-3-42	5-21-41	394,464	2,300,622	Alternating Current Generator Key
T	3-2-43	11-27-40	367,339	2,312,902	Relay, Line
T	4-6-43	6-20-39	280,042	2,316,067	Method of Threading Rolling Mill
T	7-20-43	12-30-41	424,865	2,324,623	Switching Device, Magnetic
T	4-11-44	5-21-41	394,463	2,364,305	Preset Call Transmitter Key Set
R	11-14-44	5-10-43	486,401	2,362,484	Pressure Gauge, Copper Ball
T	11-14-44	2-10-43	475,380	2,362,632	Selector Switch Escapement
R	3-11-47	5-30-44	538,063	2,417,076	High Speed Camera, Ribbon Frame
R	Not Issued	10-18-45	?	?	Separation Means
R	1-20-48	3-1-44	524,566	2,434,652	Igniter for Rocket
R	3-16-48	5-15-46	669,765	2,437,694	Method for Blending Powder Grains
M	4-6-48	11-13-44	749,644	2,439,211	Submarine Mine, Oscillating
R	4-27-48	6-26-44	542,214	2,440,271	Rocket Projectile, 4¼ inch
R	8-10-48	11-16-44	563,739	2,446,537	Thrust Gauge, Strain Gauge

T = Telephone
A = Archery
R = Rockets
P = Piano
M = Mines

	Issue Date	File Date	Serial No.	Patent No.	Subject
R	11-2-48	5-7-47	746,548	2,452,892	Igniter for Rocket, Long Type
R	1-18-49	6-1-44	538,314	2,459,163	Thermal Igniter for Rocket Flare
R	2-1-49	3-16-45	583,140	2,460,289	Rocket Projectile Control Valve
R	2-22-49	5-15-46	669,766	2,462,099	Rocket Projectile Burster Tube
R	3-8-49	9-2-43	501,002	2,464,179	Smokeless Powder Tester
R	5-31-49	3-21-46	656,118	2,471,745	Spacer Trap for Rockets
R	6-7-49	11-16-44	563,738	2,472,108	Thrust Gauge for Rockets Latteral
R	10-25-49	9-2-47	776,391	2,485,601	Multiple Cartridge Launcher, JB2
R	11-8-49	11-16-44	563,740	2,487,053	Obturator Trap for Bazooka Rocket
R	4-4-50	11-16-44	563,737	2,502,458	Trap for Propellant (Cement Type)
T	4-4-50	3-6-47	732,861	2,502,842	Electromagnetic Relay, Line Relay
R	4-11-50	6-1-44	538,316	2,503,269	Rocket Propellant Flare
R	4-11-50	11-16-44	563,735	2,503,270	Trap for Rocket Projectile, Pin Type
R	4-11-50	2-6-45	576,439	2,503,271	Rocket Projectile, Central Venturi
R	6-6-50	3-30-45	585,756	2,510,110	Step Motor, Rocket Projectile
T	7-25-50	4-10-48	20,303	2,516,772	Cross Wire Switch
R	8-22-50	5-17-45	594,241	2,519,905	Driver Rocket
R	10-19-50	8-22-46	692,155	2,522,514	Arming Device for Fuse
R	3-13-51	2-9-45	577,074	2,545,204	Jet Accelerated Armour Piercing Bomb
R	4-24-51	8-24-44	551,047	2,549,811	Powder Trap, Pin Type
T	8-14-51	7-28-49	107,156	2,564,432	Impulse Counting Relay
T	9-11-51	3-26-49	17,136	2,567,812	Code Transmitter Telephone Set
R	11-13-51	1-30-43	474,213	2,574,478	Propellant Having an Opacifier
R	1-29-52	6-28-45	602,141	2,585,570	Adjustable Nozzle for Rocket Motor
T	2-12-52	6-6-47	753,066	2,585,010	Wire Connecting Tool
R	2-19-52	11-29-44	565,644	2,586,229	Replaceable Firing Pin for 4.2 Mortar
T	3-18-52	7-3-47	758,904	2,589,806	Selective Signal System, Counting
R	5-13-52	12-10-46	715,298	2,596,644	Automatic Detachable Flashless Nozzle for Rockets
R	5-27-52	4-21-45	589,500	2,589,256	Recoilless Gun, 4.2
R	8-5-52	11-16-44	563,736	2,605,607	Trap for Rocket Propellant
R	12-9-52	11-29-44	565,645	2,620,732	Mortar Charge, 4.2
R	4-7-53	2-28-46	650,931	2,633,702	Multiple Nozzle Rocket
T	8-11-53	7-19-49	105,542	2,648,589	Magnetic Recorder
R	11-17-53	9-23-52	311,105	2,659,589	Integrating Accelerometer
R	2-8-55	5-3-52	680,306	2,701,525	Mortar Shell Loading Driver Rocket
R	11-22-55	3-5-46	652,206	2,724,237	Rocket Projectile Having Discreet Flight and Sustaining Chambers
R	7-5-60	3-27-45	585,183	2,943,673	Flame Thrower

Appendix D

CITATION TO ACCOMPANY THE AWARD OF

THE MEDAL FOR MERIT

TO

DR. CLARENCE N. HICKMAN

DR. CLARENCE N. HICKMAN, for exceptionally meritorious conduct in the performance of outstanding services to the United States from July, 1940 to June, 1946. Dr. Hickman, Chief of Section H of the Division of Rocket Ordnance of the National Defense Research Committee, Office of Scientific Research and Development, foresaw, with rare vision and with remarkable accuracy, at the outset of European hostilities and before the United States was involved in the war, the role of the rocket in modern warfare. As a rocket enthusiast since the days of the first world war and as a scientist, with experience in the field of rocketry and knowledge of how the relatively crude, early rockets might be improved, he was able to grasp their tremendous potentialities as weapons, and he was instrumental in persuading the National Defense Research Committee that a program of rocket research should be initiated. He displayed great enterprise and scientific acumen in his direction of the work of the Atlantic Coast group of investigators at the Allegany Ballistics Laboratory whose studies led to the development of powerful new weapons: the small rocket to be used by infantrymen which was effective against tanks; the jet-accelerated armor-piercing bomb; the target rocket to be used in the training of anti-aircraft gunners; the recoilless gun; and a high velocity aircraft rocket. That the rocket weapons of the United States were among the most vital and successful types of ordnance is the result in no small part of Dr. Hickman's vision and planning.

THE WHITE HOUSE

February 2, 1948.

THE UNITED STATES OF AMERICA

TO ALL WHO SHALL SEE THESE PRESENTS, GREETING:

THIS IS TO CERTIFY THAT
THE PRESIDENT OF THE UNITED STATES OF AMERICA
IN ACCORDANCE WITH THE ORDER ISSUED BY GENERAL
GEORGE WASHINGTON AT HEADQUARTERS, NEWBURGH,
NEW YORK, ON AUGUST 7, 1782, AND PURSUANT TO ACT
OF CONGRESS, HAS AWARDED THE MEDAL

FOR MERIT
TO

DR. CLARENCE N. HICKMAN

FOR EXTRAORDINARY FIDELITY AND EXCEPTIONALLY
MERITORIOUS CONDUCT

GIVEN UNDER MY HAND IN THE CITY OF WASHINGTON
THIS SECOND DAY OF FEBRUARY 1948

SECRETARY OF STATE

COMMANDER-IN-CHIEF

Appendix F

AMERICAN SCORES OF JAPANESE-AMERICAN ARCHERY CONTEST

Held in Jackson Heights, N. Y. U. S. A., October 17th 1937.

Under Auspices of The National Archery Association
Conducted by the Long Island Archers

Field Captain ----P. F. Lepanto   Referee --T. Okajima

Official Representation:

America - Dr. P. E. Klopsteg, Chairman of Board of Governors of
          The National Archery Association.
Japan   - Mr. Wakasugi, Japanese Consulate General.

Archer	Target No.	30 arrows at 40 yards			30 arrows at 31 yards		Total Score
		Hits	Score	Rank	Hits	Rank	
Harold R. Hill	4	30	224	1	19	4	243
C. J. Weese	4	30	212	2	18	5	230
E. Harold Potts	1	29	201	3	23	1	224
J. K. Chichester	7	30	200	4	23	1	223
W. L. Squires	2	28	198	5	22	2	220
Lester Rexon	3	30	196	6	11	11	207
Mrs. J. Marshall	6	29	193	7	20	3	213
Peter F. Lepanto	6	28	192	8	19	4	211
W. H. Jackson	1	29	187	9	20	3	207
C. Gray Smith	1	29	187	9	11	11	198
Lester G. Chapin	1	29	177	10	9	13	186
E. Derwood Myers	5	30	172	11	14	9	186
Miss Dorothy Budd	3	29	171	12	16	7	187
Dr. Robert P. Elmer	4	30	170	13	17	6	187
Jule F. Marshall	7	28	170	13	14	9	184
James E. Maberly	3	29	169	14	10	12	179
George Schilpp	5	29	169	14	7	15	176
Frank O. Humphreys	8	29	165	15	22	2	187
George Olsen	3	29	159	16	15	8	174
C. E. VanSiclen	8	28	158	17	12	10	170
Harold Sturr	7	28	154	18	19	4	173
O. C. Lempfert	2	28	148	19	6	16	154
Robert C. Sturm	2	28	136	20	12	10	148
Mrs. Myrtle Miller	2	22	126	21	11	11	137
J. W. Hinman	4	27	125	22	7	15	132
John A. Carlson	6	26	122	23	7	15	129
Waldron Slutter	5	27	119	24	8	14	127
Lester T. Gates	6	24	112	25	11	11	123
Robert Van Riper	5	21	103	26	10	12	113
J. R. McKay	8	23	99	27	12	10	111
Total		836	4914		425		5339
Average		27.9	163.8		14.1		178.0

C. N. Hickman   Secretary - Long Island Archers.

Appendix G

JAPANESE-AMERICAN ARCHERY CONTEST

OCTOBER   24 1937

Official scores made in Japan.

Rank	Name	Score	Address	Occupation
1.	K. Shigeno	232	3-115 Minamisenzi Arakawaku Tokyo	Liquor Dealer
2.	S. Koshimura	230	Atam Shizuokaken Japan	Archery Teach.
3.	H. Maruyama	220	10 Gokencho Kandaku Tokyo	Badge Mfg.
4.	S. Marayama	216	46 Suidomachi Koishikawaku Tokyo	Bicycle Dealer.
5.	S. Urgami	214	15 Ichigaya Ushigomeku Tokyo	Archery Teach.
6.	T. Nakano	212	4-26 Araimachi Omoriku Tokyo	Co. Clerk
7.	Hayashide	210	1-768 Kamosaki Shinagewaku Tokyo	Archery Teach.
8.	T. Murakoshi	208	2-13 Sakaedori Shibuyaku Tokyo	Attorney
8.	K. Noguchi	208	2-277 Okubo Yodobashiky Tokyo	Bow Maker
9.	T. Shikakura	202	23 Senzu Adachiku Tokyo	Chem. Mfg.
9.	M Sagawa	202	2-125 Hagikubo Suginamiku Tokyo	Co. Clerk
10.	H. Suzuki	200	1-99 Yodobashiku Tokyo	Prop. Owner
11.	R. Sudo	198	68 Shimokitasawa Setagayaku Tokyo	High School T.
12.	K. Ishibashi	194	6-349 Nippori Arakawaku Tokyo	Contractor
12.	T. Matsumoto	194	2-56 Hongodori Nakanoku Tokyo	Prop. Owner
12.	N. Inouye	194	2-602 Takata Toyoshimaku Tokyo	Dye Mfg.
13.	K. Osaka	192	4-75 Axumacho Mukojimaku Tokyo	Oron Mfg.
14.	Z. Hamada	190	8 Kurumsaka Shitayaku Tokyo	Hotel Prop.
15.	R. Shirase	189	2-207 Nishisugamo Toyoshinaku T.	Prop. Owner
16.	M. Fujisawa	188	2-4 Surugadai Kandaku Tokyo	Cival Servant
16.	M. Yamada	188	4 Nakashucho Nihonbashiku Tokyo	Laundry Owner
17.	M. Sone	187	1-879 Tsunohazu Yodobashiku T.	Bow Maker
18.	S. Kubota	186	4- Tajima Asakusaku Tokyo	Archery Teach.
18.	G. Inouye	186	23 Shinzu Adachiku Tokyo	Baker
19.	T. Shimorura	185	23 Senzu Adachiku Tokyo	Writer
20.	S. Ogasawara	184	2-40 Okajimachi Shitayaku Tokyo	Co. Clerk
21.	T. Sano	180	3-743 Nishisugamo Toyoshinaku T.	Bow Maker
22.	S. Fijiwara	165	3-3950 Minamimachi Toyshimaku T.	Prop. Owner
23.	T. Saito	156	76 Yaraicho Ushigomeku Tokyo	Attorney
24.	K. Matsui	141	2-213 Totsuka Yodobashiku Tokyo	Co. Clerk.

Total Score 5851   Received Jan. 22, 1938.

Average *   195.03

                   C. N. Hickman

          3536 79th Street

          Jackson Heights, N. Y.

American Scores

Total 4914

Av.   163.8

High   224

Low   99

Appendix H

<u>SECOND JAPANESE-AMERICAN ARCHERY TOURNAMENT SCORES</u>

Japanese tournament held in Tokio, Japan Sept. 25th 1938
American tournament at Jackson Heights, N. Y. U. S. A. Oct. 1st 1938

	Names of Archers		30 arrows at 50 yds American target				20 arrows Jap. Tar.	
			Japanese		American		Jap.	Am.
Rank	Japanese	American	H.	S.	H.	S.	31	yards
1.	K. Noguchi	Gage, Harry D.	30	204	30	210	19	17
2.	T. Matsumoto	Weese, Carl J.	30	194	30	200	14	18
3.	D. Tada	Wetherill, Proctor	29	191	30	196	17	14
4.	M. Inonye	Hill, Harold R.	30	187	30	190	12	15
5.	M. Imamura	Squire, Winfield S.	29	181	30	186	18	18
6.	S. Nakade	Morse, Lester K.	30	178	30	184	18	13
7.	T. Motonaga	Potts, E. Harold	28	176	30	178	16	16
8.	K. Shigeno	Miller, Walter L.	30	172	29	169	17	17
9.	S. Tamai	Jackson, W. H.	28	170	28	168	15	17
10.	T. Kumazawa	Humphries, Frank O.	29	165	30	164	18	15
11.	H. Shinohara	Brown, Howland S.	30	162	29	160	12	16
12.	H. Iwao	Todd, E. Murray	30	158	29	159	11	13
13.	K. Yoshikawa	Rexon, Mrs. Lester	29	157	27	155	11	9
14.	T. Egawa	McKay, J. R.	30	155	29	153	16	11
15.	P. Tamura	Booth, L. E. Jr.	27	149	27	151	17	13
16.	K. Mita	Lane, Alfred D.	30	148	28	150	12	16
17.	S. Kobayashi	Myers, E. Derwood	28	148	29	147	11	15
18.	K. Shirasu	Bolling, Miss Diana	28	146	28	144	18	7
19.	H. Maruyama	Johnson, Mrs. Claude	29	139	26	144	16	5
20.	R. Ishii	Rexon, Lester	27	139	29	143	13	7
21.	K. Makaigasa	Elmer, Dr. Robert P.	27	133	27	143	14	9
22.	K. Kihara	Sterner, William A.	26	132	26	142	15	7
23.	S. Ogasawara	Arden, Ray	28	128	26	140	15	9
24.	T. Kawaguchi	Marshall, Mrs. Jule	28	128	28	138	10	11
25.	H. Kojima	Davis, Harry E.	27	127	26	132	10	10
26.	K. Shibata	Kalligan, Miss Janet	25	121	26	118	17	9
27.	K. Yoshida	Smith, C. Gray	26	120	24	116	11	9
28.	H. Niihara	Johnson, Claude R.	25	119	24	116	14	7
29.	K. Kawata	Gates, Mrs. Lester	23	107	25	109	19	11
30.	G. Ikeda	Goeltz, William S.	20	106	23	97	7	10
	Total		836	4535	833	4605	425	357
	Average		27.9	151.2	27.8	153.5	14.2	11.7

Dr. M Koyama, Pres., Mr. T. Chiba, Sec., Mr. Y. Uno Sec.,
Mr. N. Kane ko Sec., and Mr. T. Kawaguchi Sec. of Kyushinkai.
Witnesses to Tokio Tournament: Mr. H. C. Amos--Prin. Am. School Tokio.
Mr. D. McAlpin Pyle--Hon. Attache of U. S. Embassy Tokio, Mr. S. Itoh-
Ex President and Mr. Okajima Sec. of Nippon Archers of N. Y.

Dr. P. E. Klopsteg--Chairman of Board of Gov. Nat. Archery Association
Dr. Robert P. Elmer-- Chairman of Committee on International Contests
Mr. W. H. Jackson--Chairman of Committee for selecting Archer s
Mr. E. Derwood Myers-- Field Captain, Mr. Wada Assistant Fiel Captain
Mr. G. A. Smith-- Recorder of Scores assisted by Mr. Matsuo.
Japanese Witnesses: Mr. S. Mizutani, Pres. Nippon Archers of N. Y.
Mr. Tanaka and Mr. S. Shibata.
Dr. C. N. Hickman-- Director of Tournament and Member of Committee on
International Archery Contests.

Appendix I

U. S. DEPARTMENT OF JUSTICE
Immigration and Naturalization Service
~~ExiksxIxixndzxBxYxMx~~
70 Columbus Avenue
New York 23, N. Y. File No. 99613/4913
August 26, 1943

Dr. C. H. Hickman
536- 79 Street
Jackson Heights, N. Y.

Dear Sir ~~exzkzkzx~~:

   In re:________________TATSUGORO OKAJIMA________________,Alien Enemy

        The above-named person has been apprehended as an alien
enemy and consideration is now being given to the disposition of his/
her case. If ordered paroled it will be necessary for him/her to
have a civilian sponsor, who will keep in close touch with him/her
and make periodic reports to this Service.

        Your name has been submitted to the undersigned as one who
may be willing to act as sponsor. In order that you may be familiar
with the duties and responsibilities of sponsorship there are enclosed herewith for your information, copies of (1) the standard
"Sponsor's Agreement" which a person is required to sign if he/she
is accepted as sponsor, and (2) the standard "Conduct to be Observed
by Alien Enemies" which, in addition to any special conditions im-
posed, the alien must observe.

        It will be appreciated if you will advise me whether you
are willing to accept the duties of sponsorship for this alien enemy.
If you are, please fill out in quadruplicate the "Statement of
Sponsor", submitted herewith, and promptly return all four copies in
the enclosed self-addressed envelope, which requires no postage. It
is not necessary at this time to sign the "Sponsor's Agreement." As
stated herein above it is sent to you at this time for your information only. It will be necessary to sign it only in the event that
parole is authorized and you are selected by the "Alien Enemy Hearing
Board" as sponsor.

        I have to state in this connection that performance of the
duty of sponsor is purely voluntary and can be most helpful to the
Government and your community as a patriotic contribution to the
national defense in safeguarding the public interest. Your prompt attention and cooperation in this matter will be very much appreciated.

                        Very truly yours,

                        W. F. WATKINS
                        District Director
                        New York District

                   By: _/s/_ G. S. GERMAN
                        Inspector in Charge
                        Chief District Parole Officer

Enclosures
     ec

Appendix J

CITATION TO ACCOMPANY CONFERRING OF

DOCTOR OF ARCHERY.

ON

CLARENCE N. HICKMAN

In recognition of many years of unselfish
and outstanding service to the sport of archery;
because of valuable achievements in the physical
problems associated with the sport,which have resulted in improvements in archery tackle that have
made possible improvements in scores generally;
for exceptional meritorious work in velocity and
acceleration of arrows, effeciency of bows, development of silk and Fortisan backings, for research leading to improvement in the flat bow,for
high spedd motion pictures related to the 'Archer's
Paradox', for general interest in the sport and
constant advancement in improvements in teaching
methods, for constant encouragement and assistance
to the staff of the Teela-Wooket Archery Camp;
we confer this Honarary Degree of Doctor of Archery
on Clarence N. Hickman.

Teela-Wooket Archery Camp
Roxbury,Vermont

June 27,1948.   Myrtle K.Miller

Appendix K

Fig. 99

Portrait being presented to Clarence Hickman by
Terrence Clark, artist New Mexico, 1952

Appendix L

C.N. Hickman: Memberships, Degrees, Awards (Archery)

1935   Honorary Member, Nippon Archery Club, New York City

1936   Honorary Member, North Shore Archers, Long Island, N.Y.

1939   Honorary Member, New York Archers

1946   Honorary Member, The National Archery Association

1948   Awarded degree of Doctor of Archery, Teela-Wooket
Archery School

1949   Honorary Member, Bell Telephone Laboratories Archery Club

1950   Awarded Maurice Thompson Medal of Honor by the
National Archery Association, Lancaster, Pennsylvania

1951   Honorary Member, Centre Archers, Long Island, N.Y.

1956   Honorary Member, Eastern Archery Association

1974   Honorary Member, Madison Long Bow Archery Club

1975   Certificate of Achievement from Teela-Wooket Archery School

1977   Inducted into the New York State Archery Association
Hall of Fame

1977   Inducted into the National Archery Association Hall of Fame

Long Island Archery Association, Member

Metropolitan Archery Association, Member

New Jersey Archery Association, Member

Society of Archery Antiquaries, Member

Appendix M

C.N. Hickman: Awards, Memberships

1946, May 6   Received Honorary Degree of Doctor of Science from
Clark University for World War II
Rocket Contributions

1948, Jan. 1   Made Honorary member of the Mayor's Committee
celebrating the Golden Jubilee of the City of
New York by the Mayor, William O'Dwyer.

1948, May   The Dr. C.N. Hickman Award was established by the
American Rocket Society for his contributions to the
rocket program in World War II.

1948, June 22   Received The Medal for Merit from the President of
the United States (Harry S. Truman) for his
contributions to the rocket developments in World
War II.

1954, Oct. 20   Awarded the John Price Wetherill Medal by
the Franklin Institute.

1971, Jan. 15   Received Achievement Award from the Music Box
Society for contributions to the development of the
Model B AMPICO.

1971, Aug. 19   Elected to Life Membership in the Franklin Institute.

1971, Apr.   Made Honorary Member of AMICA - Automatic
Musical Instrument Collector's Association.

National Geographic Association, Member
American Physical Society, Member
Acoustical Society of America, Member
Institute of Radio Engineers, Member
Society of Motion Picture Engineers, Member
Masonic Lodge, New Albany, Indiana, Member
Society of American Magicians, Member
International Brotherhood of Magicians, Member
Club of Pioneers, Bell Telephone Labs, Member

Appendix N

Fig. 100

Modern Tournament Bow Design Based Upon Hickman Principles

SELECTED BIBLIOGRAPHY

PRIMARY SOURCES

BOOKS

Hickman, Clarence N., Editor. *Archery Poems* by James Duff and
May Duff Murray, Privately Printed. 1956.

Hickman, Clarence N. *Genealogy of the Hickman Families of
Virginia, Kentucky, Indiana and Texas.* Jackson Heights,
N.Y.:Westminster Printing Co., 1967.

Hickman, Clarence N. *Metropolitan Archery Association History,*
1925-1950. Privately Printed. 1950.

Hickman, Clarence N.; Klopsteg, Paul; and Nagler, Forrest.
Archery, The Technical Side. Milwaukee:
North American Press, 1947.

Goddard, E. and Pendray, G., Editors. *The Papers of
Robert H. Goddard.* Volume 1, 1898-1924. New York:
McGraw Hill Book Co., 1970.

PERIODICALS

Hickman, Clarence N. "Acoustic Spectrometer."
Bell Laboratories Record. 12 (October 1934): 60-62.

_________ . "Aiming Method for Shooting Fish." *Archery.*
29 (December 1957):26-27.

_________ . "A Flexible Bow Handle." *The Archery Review.*
3 (October 1933):6-7.

_________ . "Ancient Composite Bow." *Journal of the Society of
Archer Antiquaries.* 1959. Hickman Archives

_________ . "A New Bow Sight." *The American Archer.*
2 (March 1941): 7.

__________ . "A Portable Spark Chronograph for Use on Either Director or Alternating Current." *Journal of the Franklin Institute*. 211 (January 1931):59-65.

__________ . "Archery for Losers." *The American Archer*. 6 (1940):5-7,11.

__________ . "Arrow Poisons for Modern Surgery." *Journal of The Society of Archer Antiquaries*. 1 (March 1958). Hickman Archives.

__________ . "A Tribute to Charles Fuller Stoddard." *The Amica*. 16 (August/September 1979): 145-147.

__________ . "A Tribute to Charles Fuller Stoddard." Part II. *The Amica*. (October 1979):169-171.

__________ . "A Variable Resistor of Low Value." *Journal of the Optical Society of America*. 6 (October 1922): 848-851.

__________ . "A Week at Teela-Wooket." *Archery*. 18 (October 1946):7.

__________ . "Bent Bow Measurements." *American Bowman Review*. (February 1938):20. Hickman Archives.

__________ . "Big Chief Charlie Norton Goes to Happy Hunting Grounds." *American Bowman Review*. (April 1940):31. Hickman Archives

__________ . "Bows and Arrows." *Safety Education*. 28 (May 1949):8-9.

__________ . "Carp Shooting on the Rio Grande." *The Archer's Magazine*. 2 (May 1953):17.

__________ . "Chains for Bows." *American Archer*. 1 (January 1940):15-16.

__________ . "Critical Bows." *The Archer's Magazine*. (July 1955): 10. Hickman Archives.

__________ . "Delayed Speech." *Bell Laboratories Record*. 2 (June 1933):308-310.

________. "Effect of Bow Length on Static Strains and Stresses."
Ye Sylvan Archer. (August 1931). Hickman Archives.

________. "Effect of Bracing Height of Bows on Static Strains and
Stresses." *Ye Sylvan Archer*.
(March 1931). Hickman Archives.

________. "Effect of Permanent Set and Reflexing of Bows on Static
Strains and Stresses" *Ye Sylvan Archer*.
(May 1931):3-5. Hickman Archives.

________. "Effect of Rigid Middle Section of Bow on Static Strains
and Stresses." *Ye Sylvan Archer*.
(February 1931):5-8. Hickman Archives.

________. "Effect of String Weight on Arrow Velocity and Efficiency
of Bows." *Ye Sylvan Archer*.
(April 1931). Hickman Archives.

________. "Effect of the Center of Gravity of An Arrow on Its
Flight." *The Archery Review*.
(February 1934): 10-11. Hickman Archives.

________. "Effect of Thickness and Width of a Bow on Its Form of
Bending." *Ye Sylvan Archer*.
(January 1932). Hickman Archives.

________. "Effect of Weight and Air Resistance of Bow Tips on Cast
of a Bow." *Ye Sylvan Archer*.
(September 1931). Hickman Archives.

________. "Fiber Stresses in Bows." *Ye Sylvan Archer*.
(March 1932). Hickman Archives.

________. "Fortisan for Backing Bows." *Archery*.
18 (March 19467):22.

________. "Fortisan for Backing Bows." *American Bowman-Review*.
15 (March 1946):4.

________. "Freezing Analyzed." *The Archer's Magazine*.
7 (December 1958):5-10.

________ . "Freezing--Some Causes, Preventions, and Cures." *American Bowman-Review*. 2 (August 1941):7-9.

________ . "General Formulas for Static Strains and Stresses in Drawing a Bow." *Ye Sylvan Archer*. (November 1930):5-9. Hickman Archives.

________ . "How the Ancient Bowman Aimed." *The Archer's Magazine*. (April 1956). Hickman Archives.

________ . "Index to Volumes 1-2-3, August 1931 to August 1934." *The Archery Review*. (July 1935):2-8. Hickman Archives.

________ . "Indoor Targets." *The Archery Review*. 2 (May 1933):3-4.

________ . "Indoor Target Faces." *The Archery Review*. 2 (April 1933):10.

________ . "Japanese-American Archery Contests." *The Archery Review*. 3 (March 1934):7-8.

________ . "Magnetic Recording and Reproducing." *Bell Laboratories Record*. 16 (September 1937): 2-6.

________ . "Portable Bow-Bracing Jig." *The Archer's Magazine*. 7(August 1958):14-17.

________ . "Reversing the Cock Feather." *The British Archer*. (February 1959).

________ . "Sound Recording on Magnetic Tape." *The Bell System Technical Journal*. 16 (April 1937):165-177.

________ . "Spark Chronograph Developed for Measuring the Intensity of Percussion Instrument Tones." *Acoustical Journal*. (October 1929):138-146. Hickman Archives.

________ . "Striking Force of a Hunting Arrow." *The Archer's Magazine*. (June 1959). Hickman Archives.

________ . "The Dynamics of a Bow and Arrow." *Journal of Applied Physics*. 8 (June 1937): 404-409.

________ . "The Neutral Plane of Bending of a Bow."
Ye Sylvan Archer. (February 1932):3-5.
Hickman Archives.

________ . "There is No Such Thing as A New Card Trick." *M.U.M.*
55 (June 1965). Hickman Archives.

________ . "Velocity and Acceleration of Arrows, Weight and
Efficiency of Bows as Affected by Backing of Bow."
Journal of the Franklin Institute. 208 (October
1929):522-523.

________ . "Ye Sylvan Archer Index, 1935-1943." Vol. 7, No. 8 to
Vol. 15, No. 8, (December 1943). Hickman Archives.

________ . "Why the Young Adults are Shooting in Phoenix."
The Archer's Magazine. 7 (July 1958):15-16.

MANUSCRIPTS

Hickman, Clarence N. "A Brief Historical Account of the Development
of the Fins for the 4½" Army Rockets." May 30, 1944.
Hickman Archives.

________ . "A Description of a New Grand Piano Action and
Comparisons with Present Grand Piano Action." Research
Laboratory, American Piano Company, N.Y.
November 5, 1928. Hickman Archives.

________ . "A Mechanical Device for the Study and Design of Bows."
July 1932. Hickman Archives.

________ . "A Method for Determining the Natural Frequency of
Wood." No date. Hickman Archives.

________ . "A New Bow--Unique in Shape and Performance."
March 5, 1935. Hickman Archives.

________ . "An Improved Bow Limb." January 29, 1935.
Hickman Archives.

________ . "Anti-Freeze Tests." February 19, 1948.
Hickman Archives.

__________ . "An 8mm Camera with Variable Speeds of from 200 to 6000 Frames per Second." December 8, 1942. Hickman Archives.

__________ . "Archery Activities in New Mexico, 1951-1953." Hickman Archives.

__________ . "Archery Activities of C.N. Hickman." August 1954. Hickman Archives.

__________ . "Archery Hints." No date. Hickman Archives.

__________ . "Archery Is My Hobby." No date. Hickman Archives.

__________ "A Short History of Archery." No date. Hickman Archives.

__________ . "A Tribute to Charles Fuller Stoddard, Inventor of the Ampico Reproducing Piano, and Director of The American Piano Company Research Laboratory." Original Full draft of a Speech Given to the Automatic Musical Instrument Collectors Association Covention, Philadelphia, PA. June 30, 1979. Hickman Archives.

__________ . "Backing Materials for Bows." November 12, 1938. Hickman Archives.

__________ . "Bell Telephone Laboratories Club, 1932-1950." Hickman Archives.

__________ . "Bow Weighing and Plotting Machine." April 1938. Hickman Archives.

__________ . "Breaking Strength of Fiber." January 9, 1948. Hickman Archives.

__________ . "Clarence N. Hickman's 85th Birthday and Christian D. Kutchinski's 52nd Wedding Anniversary." August 18, 1974. Hickman Archives.

__________ . "Classification of Cross-Bows Based on Work Done in Drawing." No date. Hickman Archives.

__________ . "Code to 13 Records of Bow Movements." No date. Hickman Archives.

__________ . "Deflection of Three Vaned Arrow." July 22, 1956. Hickman Archives.

__________ . "Eastern Archery Association, 1937-1956." Hickman Archives.

__________ . "Effect of Archer's Height on Location of Point-of-Aim." November 19, 1947. Hickman Archives.

__________ . "Extracts from *Bell Laboratories Record* Pertaining to C.N.H. Activities." 1930-1950. Hickman Archives.

__________ . "Form of Bending and Free Period of a Round Rod Clamped at One End." No date. Hickman Archives.

__________ . "Form of Bending of Triangular Shaped Springs." February 24, 1947. Hickman Archives.

__________ . "Highlights in the Life of Clarence N. Hickman." October 15, 1980.

__________ . "Jackson Heights Archers--1928-1941." Hickman Archives.

__________ . "Japanese-American Archery Contest Rules." October 1937. Hickman Archives.

__________ . "Japanese-American Archery Contests--Correspondence, Scores, Beginning 1937." Hickman Archives.

__________ . "Kinetic Energy of a Bow String for 100% Efficiency of Bow." May 15, 1947. Hickman Archives.

__________ . "Long Island Archers--Tournaments, Correspondence, Notices, 1931-1941." Hickman Archives.

__________ . "Memories of Association with Dr. Robert H. Goddard." November 8, 1975. Hickman Archives.

__________ . "Metropolitan Archery Association--Silver Anniversary Year." 1950. Hickman Archives.

________ . "Metropolitan Archery Association--Programs, Clippings, Scores, Correspondence, 1928." Hickman Archives.

________ . "New York Archers--Notices, Correspondence, Point-of-Aim." Beginning May 1938. Hickman Archives.

________ . "Notes on A HISTORY OF THE ROYAL TOXOPHILITE SOCIETY From Its Institution to the Present Time--Edited by a Toxophilite in 1867". . .With Additions Bringing the History up to October 1944. Hickman Archives.

________ . "Plastics for Archery." 1946. Hickman Archives.

________ . "Silk Backing for Bows." No date. Hickman Archives.

________ . "Stability of Featherless Arrows." No date. Hickman Archives.

________ . "The Deceleration of An Arrow Due to Air Resistance." No date. Hickman Archives.

________ . "The Flat Bow in Theory and Practice." January 1940. Hickman Archives.

________ . "Trajectory of Arrow Having a Small Angle of Departure." No date. Hickman Archives.

________ . "The Free Period of a Bow." No date. Hickman Archives.

________ . "Trajectory of Arrow Having a Small Angle of Departure." No date. Hickman Archives

________ . "Two, Three and Four Plastic Vanes for Arrows Configuration, Stabilization and Tests." September 15, 1954. Hickman Archives.

CORRESPONDENCE

Elmer, Dr. Robert. Letter to Hickman, C.N. April 20, 1945. Hickman Archives.

Hamilton, Max. Letter to Anderson, J.W., Editor. *The Archer's Magazine.* December 27, 1958.

Hibbard, John. Letter to Hickman, C.N. July 20, 1961.
Hickman Archives.

Hickman, C.N. Letter to J.W. Anderson, January 3, 1959.
Hickman Archives.

__________ . Letter to John P. Craven, Chief Scientist, Department of
the Navy, July 18, 1961. Hickman Archives.

__________ . Letter to Paul Crouch, April 14, 1962.
Hickman Archives.

__________ . Letter to Mrs. Ruth Dick, Secretary, Eastern Archery
Association, June 14, 1962. Hickman Archives.

__________ . Letter to Dr. Harvey Fletcher, February 3, 1965.
Hickman Archives

__________ . Letter to John B. Hibbard, Chairman of NAA Eligibility
Committee, July 8, 1961. Hickman Archives.

__________ . Letter to John B. Hibbard, Harrisburg, Pa.
September 10, 1961. Hickman Archives.

__________ . Letter to Earl Hoyt Jr. May 11, 1961. Hickman Archives.

__________ . Letter to Earl Hoyt Jr. "Comments on Significant
Advancements in Modern Bow Design." July 31, 1961.
Hickman Archives.

__________ . Letter to W.H. Jackson, Robin Hood Archery Company,
N.J. March 8, 1949. Hickman Archives.

__________ . Letter to Dr. F.B. Jewett, President of National Academy
of Sciences and Bell Telephone, "An Investigation
Pertaining to Rockets." June 20, 1940. Hickman Archives.

__________ . Letter to Paul Klopsteg, Glenview, Ill. April 15, 1962.
Hickman Archives.

__________ . Letter to John Mills, April 4, 1940. Hickman Archives.

__________. Letter to Frederick I. Ordway, III., Director, General
     Astronautics Research Corporation, Washington, D.C.
     (Supplying Material to be used for a manuscript on the
     history of rocketry and astronautics.). February 2, 1966.
     Hickman Archives.

__________. Letter to Charles Pierson, December 9, 1959.
     Hickman Archives.

__________. Letter to C.A. Saunders, March 26, 1966.
     Hickman Archives.

__________. Letter to George Suddell, Eastman Kodak Stores, Inc.
     September 11, 1946. Hickman Archives.

Hoyt, Earl Jr., President, Hoyt Archery Company. Letter to
     Hickman, C.N. January 29, 1959. Hickman Archives.

Hoyt, Earl Jr. Letter to Hickman, C.N. May 9, 1961. Hickman Archives.

Itoh, S., Yokohama, Japan. Letter to Hickman, C.N. May 23, 1937.
     Hickman Archives.

Jewett, F.B. Letter to Major General C.M. Wesson, Chief of Ordnance,
     Washington, D.C. July 1940. Hickman Archives.

Klopsteg, Paul E., NAA Board of Governors. Letter to Hickman, C.N.
     September 7, 1937. Hickman Archives.

Miller, Myrtle K. Letter to Hickman, C.N. September 22, 1955.
     Hickman Archives.

Munro, D.F., Professor of Modern Languages, Kansas State University.
     Letter to Hickman, C.N. December 13, 1958.
     Hickman Archives.

Nagler, Forrest, Letter to Hickman, C.N. January 22, 1946.
     Hickman Archives.

Saunders, C.A., Saunders Archery Company. Letter to
     Hickman, C.N. March 15, 1966. Hickman Archives.

PROCEEDINGS AND REPORTS

Ampico Corporation. *Service Manual.* (New York: Ampico, 1929):3,4.
Hickman Archives.

Eastern Archery Association. "77th Anniversary Tournament Results,
July 3-7, 1956." Springfield, Massachusetts.

Hickman, Clarence N. "Alternating-Current Resistance and Inductance
of Single-Layer Coils." *Scientific Papers of the Bureau of
Standards.* Washington, D.C.:Department of Commerce.
1923):73-104.

__________ . "A New Technique for Making Objects Invisible."
Presentation Before the Society of American Magicians.
Washington Assembly No. 23, June 13, 1944.
Hickman Archives.

__________ . "Ballistic Measurements and Performance of Rockets."
Talk given by Hickman at a preliminary exhibition and
demonstration for the renegotiation committee.
July 6, 1945. Hickman Archives.

__________ . "Problems and Accomplishments on Contract
OEMsr-256." Memorandum for File. November 2, 1946.
Hickman Archives.

Ives, James E., and Hickman, Clarence N. "A Study of the Oscillations
Occurring in the Circuits of the Pliotron." *Proceedings of the
Institute of Radio Engineers.* (June 1921):1-14.

Joint Board on Scientific Information Policy, Office of Scientific
Research and Development, War Department and Navy
Department. *U.S. Rocket Ordnance--Development and Use in
World War II.* March 30, 1946. Hickman Archives.

Long Island Archers Fall Tournament Program, October 15-16, 1932.
Hickman Archives.

National Archery Association. "A Brief Clarification of Pertinent
Subjects for Amateur Archery Competition." Chicago, Ill.
July 24, 1961.

National Archery Association. "Regulations Governing Amateur
Competition." Approved January 21, 1961.

The Amica. Program for Association convention. "Clarence Hickman--
Honored Guest." Philadelphia, Pa. June 2-June 3, 1979.
Hickman Archives.

Thompson, L.T.E., Hickman, C.N., and Riffolt, N. "The Measurement
of Small Time Intervals and Some Applications, Principally
Ballistic." *Proceedings of the National Academy of Science.*
6 (April 15, 1920) 169-178.

PHOTOGRAPHS

Hickman, Clarence N. "The Archer's Paradox." 16mm Film, 1937.
Hickman Archives.

_________ . "Miscellaneous Photographs of Rockets, Mortars,
Recoilless Guns, Anti-Mine Devices, Flame Throwers and
Other Devices Developed by Section H, Division 3,
NDRC, 1940-1946." Hickman Archives.

_________ . Personal Photos of Clarence Hickman. Hickman Archives.

_________ . Photos of Japanese-American Archery Contest,
Jackson Heights, N.Y. 1938. Hickman Archives.

_________ . "Photos of Archery Hour Information--Bell Laboratories
File." 1932-1950. Hickman Archives.

_________ . Photos of Spark Apparatus Used for Testing Shotgun
Charges. Hickman Archives.

Memorial Album of Japanese American Archery Tournament, Tokyo,
Japan. October 24, 1937. Hickman Archives.

The World Archery Center Photo File, Marshalls Creek, Pa.

INTERVIEWS

Hickman, Clarence, Taped interviews and transcription, in possession of
        writer, Jackson Heights, N.Y. September 10, 1979 and
        The World Archery Center, Pennsylvania, 1976-1980.

Hoyt, Ann Weber, interviewed at Colorado Springs, Co., 1980, and
        telephone interview October 1982.

<u>SECONDARY SOURCES</u>

<u>BOOKS</u>

Baier, Patricia; Bowers, Julia; Fowkes, Bud; and Schoch, Sherwood.
        NAA Instructor's Manual. 2nd Edition, 1976.

Barnes, Gladeon M. *Weapons of World War II*. New York:
        D. Van Nostrand Co. Inc..1947.

Elmer, Robert P. *Archery*. Philadelphia: Penn Publishing Co., 1926.

________ . *Target Archery*. New York: Alfred A. Knopf, 1946.

Givens, Larry. *Re-enacting the Artist--A Story of the Reproducing Piano*.
        New York: Vestal Press, 1970.

Heath, E.B. *The Grey Goose Wing*. Connecticut:
        New York Graphic Society, Ltd., 1971.

Hochman, Louis. *The Complete Archery Book*. New York:
        Arco Publishing Co, 1965.

Hodgkin, Adrian. *The Archer's Craft*. New York: A.S. Barnes, 1968.

Lambert, Arthur W. *Modern Archery*. New York: A.S. Barnes, 1932.

Longman, C.J. and Walrond, Col. H. *Archery*. London:
        Longmans, Green & Co., 1901.

Office of Scientific Research and Development. *Rocket Fundamentals*,
        The George Washington University, 1944.

Parker, Clement. *Compendium of Works on Archery*. First Edition.
     Philadelphia: McManus, 1950.

Pope, Saxton. *Bows and Arrows. Los Angeles:
     University of California Press, 1962.*

Rhode, Robert. *History of the National Archery Association 1879-1945*.
     Volume 1, Michigan: McNaughton and Gunn, 1978.

__________ . *History of the National Archery Association 1946-1978*.
     Volume 2. Michigan: McNaughton and Gunn, 1979:
     746-748.

Rounseville, Phillip. *Archery Simplified*. New York:
     A.S. Barnes and Co., 1937.

Thompson, J. Maurice. *The Witchery of Archery*. North Carolina:
     The Archers Company, 1928.

Webster's New Collegiate Dictionary. Massachusetts:
     G & C Merriam Co., 1979.

PERIODICALS

American Bowman-Review. 2 (August 1941):22.

American Bowman-Review. 15 (March 1946):inside back cover.

Bell Laboratories Record. "C.N. Hickman Commended for Rocket
     Research Work." (November, 1946). Hickman Archives.

Bell Laboratories Record. "C.N. Hickman and H.E. Ives Awarded
     Medals for Merit." 26 (August 1948):345.

Bell Laboratories Record. "C.N. Hickman Retires."
     (January 1950):37-39.

Bell Telephone Magazine. "Rocket Researcher."
     23 (February 1945):37-39.

Bell Laboratories Record. "Rocket Spinner." 24 (May 1946):183-84.

Bell Laboratories Record. "The Archery Hour." (December 1949):460.
     Hickman Archives.

Bell Laboratories Record. "The Bell System at the New York World's Fair." (September 1939) Hickman Archives.

Bell Laboratories Record. "The Mirrorphone." 20 (September 1941):2-5.

Chaklai, Morris and Rechtschaffen, Allan. "Science Hits the Bull's Eye." *Popular Mechanics Magazine.* 91 (March 1949):174-177.

Cushman, R.A. "Audition Demonstration." *Bell Laboratories Record.* (May 1940):273-277.

Cushman, R.A. "Weather Announcing Tape Machine." *Bell Laboratories Record.* (November 1939):70-71. Hickman Archives.

Ford, Horace A., Esq. "Archery, Its Theory and Practice." *The Field*, 6 (October 6, 1855). Hickman Archives.

Gibson, R.E. "Personal Reflections on the Origins of the Chemical Propulsion Information Agency." *CPIA Bulletin.* 7 (October 1981):1-4.

Huck, Helene. "Dr. Clarence N. Hickman--His Contribution to Archery." *The Archer's Magazine.* 3 (October 1954):3-5.

Jones, Phillip. "Bell Laboratories Role in Victory." *Bell Telephone Magazine.* (Spring 1946):37-72. Hickman Archives.

Kim, Boris F. "Understanding Bow Performance." *Archery International. 2 (June/July 1981):36-39.*

Klopsteg, Paul. "Archery Reflections and Observation." Archer's Magazine. (May 1968):6,46-47. Hickman Archives.

__________ . "Photographing the Paradox." *The Archery Review.* 2 (April 1933):12-13.

__________ . "Physics of Bow and Arrows." *American Journal of Physics.* 2 (August 1943):175-192.

__________ . "Roving Reminiscences and Random Recollections." *The Archer's Magazine.* (February 1974):32-36. Hickman Archives.

Krich, Charles. "TWAC's 40th Anniversary." *Archery World*.
(July 1977):22. Hickman Archives.

Reck, F.R. "The Ribbon-Frame Camera." *Bell Laboratories Record*. 23
(February 1945):40-45.

Rhode, Robert. "The Archery Hall of Fame--The Scientists."
Archery International. 2 (April 1981):40.

Schuyler, Keith. "From Arrowheads to Atomic Missiles--
Dr. Clarence N. Hickman." *Pennsylvania Game News*. 51
(December 1980):54-57.

Siegmund, H.O. "Multiple Tube Rocket Launchers." *Bell Laboratories
Record*. 24 (February 1946):49-52.

The Archer's Magazine. "Franklin Institute's John Price Wetherill Medal
Awarded to Dr. Clarence N. Hickman." 3 (October 1954):2-3.

The American Archer. "Hall of Fame." 3 (1979):5.

The Feathered Shaft. "Pictorially Speaking." 1 (June 1947):14-15.

Werolin, Alf E. "Clarence N. Hickman--New Honorary Member."
The Amica. 13 (June 1976):91-92.

NEWSPAPERS

"Book Collection Donated to Library." *Bloomington Tribune*.
January 14, 1968.

Carroll, Bill. "Physicist Likes Archery, Not to Win, But to Study."
NEW ERA, Lancaster, Pa. August 21, 1958.

Greene, Elinor. " 'Tell' Adopts Science in Archery."
New York Sunday News. July 24, 1955.

"Hoosier's Dream Was Space Aid." Indianapolis News. July 31, 1969.

"Dr. Hickman to Address Falcon Archers Meeting."
Quency Patriot Ledger. September 24, 1959.

"*Rocket Men.*" *Newsweek*. 27 (December 16, 1946).

Shapes, Jeff. "Happiness is Being a Straight Arrow."
    New York Daily News. July 17, 1977.

MANUSCRIPTS

McKensie, Daniel. "Brief History of the Metropolitan Archery
    Association." 1938. Hickman Archives.

Morey, Dr. Loren. *The Powder Rockets (1917-1942)--A History of Solid
    Fuel Rocket Development*. Copy of original manuscript.
    Hickman Archives.

Teela-Wooket Archery Camp Brochure. June 1949. Hickman Archives.